THE REFORMATION IN DUBLIN

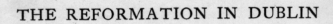

FOREWORD.

WHATEVER work has been done on this period is practically confined to Protestant historians whose books have been spoiled by lamentable bigotry. I sincerely hope I have not soiled any of my pages in any similar manner. My main object has been to gather together all available documents from the State Papers, published and unpublished, and from other reliable sources. The reader must have patience with them. It would have been much easier for me to have written a more popular book, but then it would have been less valuable. No work so far has dealt exhaustively with these documents. But it must not be supposed that I claim anything like finality. Such is not to be expected in a work of this kind. Until the Papal Registers are brought up to date we must be content with one-sided information. Had we from the pen of a contemporary in Dublin anything like Bishop Bale's *Vocacyon* (of Ossory) we should be able to get a little colouring into the picture. However, the intelligent reader will be able to supplement the tale told by the documents. Very little comment is necessary, and whatever is made is given simply and tersely, and, I hope, is justified by the documents. I find it necessary to call attention here to Robert Ware's *Life of Archbishop Browne* (*Harleian Miscellany*, Vol. V.). In reality it is just a collection in twenty pages of a few letters, etc., purporting to be Browne's. It was printed in London and in Dublin in the year 1681. This compilation has been taken, as containing genuine documents, by important historians, such as Cox (1689), Harris (1745), Leland (1814), Monck Mason (1820), Mant (1840), Bagwell (1885), and by the *National Biographical Dictionary*. King has also inserted some of them in his *Collectanea*. Although at first I took these documents seriously, and showed in my text that they were inconsistent with facts that were unknown to Robert Ware, and indeed showed that they were spurious, I now consider that it would be waste of space to include them in this history. I have accordingly cut them out completely, and consider Robert Ware a forger, and not worthy of the name of historian. I am glad to see that Fr. T. E. Bridgett (*Blunders and Forgeries*) has come to the same conclusion from a different standpoint. It is only just, however, to give here some reasons for this attitude. Briefly, they are as follows.

The forgeries of Robert Ware began in 1678 contemporaneously with the revelations of Titus Oates, and continued for some years. At first they were anonymous, but afterwards, when Ware saw they were in favour, he fathered them, for they had won credit for the monstrous stories of the " Popish Plot." The success of Ware's forgeries during two centuries was mostly due to their adoption by the historian Strype, and the great historians mentioned above have all unquestioningly accepted them. Robert Ware traded on the name of his illustrious father, Sir James Ware, and professed to draw from his father's collections. He made a parade of the high sources from which his father, according to his story, had received the various items, as, for instance, from Sir Robert Cotton, Archbishop Ussher, etc. But unfortunately for Ware, some of these items are not to be found in the places mentioned. Others are there, but they have been inserted by Ware. The collections of Sir J. Ware, formerly known as the Clarendon MSS., are now among the Additional Manuscripts, British Museum.

The documents that I consider spurious and which I have discarded are : (1) Browne's Letter to Cromwell, September, 1535 ; (2) Browne's Speech in Parliament, May, 1536 ; (3) Browne to Cromwell, 8 April, 1538 ; (4) Browne to Cromwell, May, 1538 ; (5) Order of 6 February, 1551, to Lord Deputy St. Leger, to introduce the Liturgy into Ireland ; (6) Browne's Sermon, 29 March, 1551 ; (7) Dispute between Primate Dowdall and St. Leger, March, 1551 ; (8) Dispute between Dowdall and Staples at St. Sepulchre's, May, 1551 ; (9) Conference between Dowdall, Staples, and Lord Deputy Crofts in June, 1551 ; (10) the story of Dr. Cole.

(1) Browne was not archbishop at that time ; by no possible juggling can the dates be reconciled. The letter is a tissue of absolute absurdities of which Browne could scarcely be guilty.

(2) Browne was still in England in May, 1536, and therefore could not have made this celebrated speech in the Dublin Parliament of that date. Robert Ware says that Sir James Ware copied the speech from a letter of Brabazon to Cromwell preserved in the library of Sir Robert Cotton. There is no such letter in that library, nor has it been discovered anywhere else.

(3) The contents of this letter about the removal of images and relics of saints from the Dublin Cathedrals are of a piece with letter (1), several paragraphs being almost identical in their terms

and their abuse. It is extremely improbable that Basnet, Dean of St. Patrick's, would have opposed the removal of images from his cathedral.

(4) This letter deals with a supposed commission from the Pope to the Irish people, and contains a form of oath to be taken by the people to be obedient to the Holy See and to resist heretics. Ware also gives an account of a Franciscan friar, afterwards hanged, on whom certain papers were found, among which was one supposed to come from a certain " Episcopus Metensis " (whoever that bishop is) to " My Son O'Neal," calling on that northern chieftain to suppress heresy, and quoting a prophecy of " one St. Laserianus, an Irish Bishop of Cashel " (*sic*).

(5) This is supposed to be the Order of Edward VI. Intrinsically, it is absurd, and makes Edward attribute to Henry VIII statements that the astute monarch was never guilty of.

(6) Browne's sermon in Christ Church on Easter Sunday, 1551, when the service was celebrated in Ireland for the first time according to the New Liturgy, is full of the most glaring nonsense and distortions. It shows Browne as prophesying the future of the Jesuits ! A more impudent forgery could scarcely be imagined.

(7) This represents Lord Deputy St. Leger as disputing the Mass with Dowdall. Now St. Leger was a friend of Dowdall, and also was opposed to doctrinal reform. His attitude was the very opposite to that given in this dispute.

(8) and (9) are simply dialogues between Dowdall and Staples, so constructed as to give Staples an opportunity of scoring over Dowdall in disputes about the Mass and the Pope's authority. Dowdall is made to cut a sorry figure indeed. The dialogues are full of historical and doctrinal inaccuracies, which neither Dowdall nor Staples would likely be guilty of.

(10) This story, given on the word of Archbishop Ussher, represents Dr. Cole, Dean of St. Paul's, sent to Ireland with a commission from Queen Mary for the persecution of the Protestants in Ireland ; telling his secret to the innkeeper at Chester, where he broke his journey ; letter taken out of Cole's leather box, and a pack of cards substituted, the knave of clubs uppermost ; consternation at Dublin Castle when the box was opened ; a new commission asked for and received by Cole ; an unfavourable wind preventing Cole from again taking ship to Dublin ; news that Mary had died ; and so " God preserved the Protestants in Ireland." The story is incredible, even on the supposed authority of Ussher.

An extraordinary feature of these forgeries is that Ware did not succeed in discovering any of Browne's genuine letters now preserved in the Public Record Office, London, and, of course, the originals of the forged ones have never appeared, except in Ware's *Life of Browne*. Moreover, the signature to the forged letters is given as " George Browne," whereas in the genuine letters Browne signs himself " George Dublin," which is the usual official style. Only in one case in his genuine letters does he subscribe himself " George Browne," and that is in a letter to Cromwell prior to his departure to Dublin to take up his duties as archbishop. I give the reasons for that signature in the text.

I acknowledge with great pleasure my indebtedness to the officials of the various libraries, Trinity College, National Library, Marsh's Library, Gilbert Library, Charleville Mall, British Museum, and Public Record Office, London. I have also to thank Mr. Marsh Thompson of London for his transcription of the Latin Roll of the Extent of the Religious Houses in Dublin at the Suppression, an abridgment of which is now published for the first time. Lastly, I return my sincere thanks to Fr. Gogarty for his valuable service in reading over the MS., and for his useful suggestions.

MYLES V. RONAN.

DUN LAOGHAIRE,
   19th July, 1926.

CONTENTS.

PART I.

EVE OF THE " REFORMATION " IN DUBLIN.

Browne an English Augustinian Friar—Henry's Second Marriage ; Browne's Assistance—Oxford and Cambridge Confer Doctorate on Browne—Browne, Visitor-General of Friaries—Browne, Master-General of Religion—Cromwell and Cranmer discuss Doctrinal Matters—Browne's Sermons on Purgatory—Browne appointed Archbishop of Dublin—Parliament at Dublin—Acts for the " King's Advantage and the Common Weal "—Act of Succession and of Absentees—Repeal of Poyning's Act—Act authorising the King to be Supreme Head of the Church in Ireland—Act of Appeals—Browne about to set out for Dublin—Council of Ireland ; Jealousy and Distrust—Gray secures Treaties with Irish Chiefs—Subjection of Ireland—Browne Accuses Brabazon of Fraud—Acts still Unpassed—The King's Rebuke—The King asks Browne for Ballymore—St. Patrick's Cathedral grants First Fruits—Spiritual Lords refuse to Legislate—The King's Commission—The King Rebukes Browne for Neglect—Act against Proctors in Parliament—Act against Authority of Bishop of Rome—Act for First Fruits—Act for the Twentieth Part—Act for the English Order, Habit, and Language—Act for Suppression of Religious Houses—Act for Probate of Testaments—Act for Faculties—Act of Leases—Browne's Confession of Failure as a " Reformer "—Failure throughout Leinster—Franciscans lead the Opposition—The " Form of the Beads ; " Browne's Pastoral—The Prebendaries Oppose Browne's Scheme—Browne claims Money for Promoting to Deanery—Browne " Maligned ; " Gray his " Heavy Lord "—The Battle of the Sermons ; Browne and Staples attack each other—Official Inquiry into the Sermons—Staples works for the Supremacy ; " Nearly Loses his Life "—Browne Defends Himself against Staples—Browne makes Peace with Staples—Browne denies Intention to Destroy Images and Relics—Gray Prays before the Image of Trim—Browne Burns the " Baculus Jesu "—Browne Denounces Observants and " Rome Runners "—Browne Preaches in the South—Gray Deprives Browne of his Palace—Browne promises to have the " Word of God " Preached in the Irish Tongue . *Page* I

PART II.

SUPPRESSION OF RELIGIOUS HOUSES.

PART III.

" REFORM."

INTRODUCTION.

In order that this book may be intelligible to all readers, it will be necessary to survey the organisation of the Church in Ireland before Henry VIII came to the throne, and also before he broke off relations with the Holy See.

Before the coming of the Anglo-Normans to this country bishops were, as a rule, elected to their sees by the priests and people of each diocese severally. No lay ruler had any right or privilege of presentation or of confirmation. The spiritualities and the temporalities of a see were freely controlled by the occupants, and, in time of vacancy in a see, by ecclesiastical administrators. Ecclesiastical courts from time immemorial had their rights independent of any lay ruler. It was not until Henry II., having drawn up the constitutions of Clarendon for England, sought to impose them upon Ireland, that the Church here found itself being organised in terms of feudal law. The first instance of interference by the King was his appointment of Augustine, an Irishman, to the See of Waterford in 1175, at the Council of Windsor. On that occasion Henry bade Laurence, Archbishop of Dublin, have the new bishop consecrated by Donat, Archbishop of Cashel.

This early assumption of power in the appointment of bishops to Irish Sees occurred before the Lateran Council of 1179. To that Council went Laurence with five or six other Irish bishops, but before they were allowed to depart from the shores of England they were compelled to take an oath before the King that they would do nothing at the Council detrimental to the dignity and authority of Henry. Evidently the King was uneasy about his exercise of this usurped power. But this did not prevent Laurence from laying before the Pope the whole question of the liberties of the Irish Church. As a result of the interview, Laurence was appointed Papal Legate, and worked, during the remaining short period of his life, in support of those liberties. We cannot help but think that the case of Augustine of Waterford, indicative of Henry's new rôle, was uppermost in the mind of Laurence. But

Laurence's office and his carrying out of it brought him under Henry's suspicion. Even Giraldus Cambrensis admits this, and the *Vita Secunda* of St. Laurence states that the Archbishop was " sent into exile by the persecution of the English." It was not for anything connected with King Roderick O'Connor that Laurence was forbidden by Henry to leave from any English or Welsh port, but simply because of the Archbishop's fight for the liberties of the Church of Ireland. And when Laurence, defying the prohibition, set out for Normandy in pursuit of the King, and died on his way, his object was to fight out the question with the English King.

When Laurence had gone to his reward, Henry showed immediately what his purpose was. No election of a successor was permitted to the clergy and people of Dublin, but Henry, acting on the constitutions of Clarendon, summoned some of the clergy over to England, and, proposing to them the name of John Comin, an English ecclesiastical lawyer, had, after a mock election, Comin appointed. Moreover, during the vacancy in the see, Henry appointed his own officials to take the temporalities into the King's hand. Even were Adrian's Bull proved to be spurious, yet all this was in direct violation of the clause in that document which decreed the inviolability of the rights of the Irish Church, and which was sanctioned at the time by the King. But Henry had now marked out the lines for himself and his successors in dealing with Irish Sees under his influence, and these subsequently received papal approval. Comin went to Rome to be consecrated, and, his successors having been sanctioned by successive kings, were proposed to the Popes for appointment.

The newly established procedure in filling vacancies in Irish Sees was usually as follows : On the death of the incumbent, the canons sent two of their number to the King to announce the vacancy and to ask for the licence to elect. These having returned to their diocese and announced the licence, the canons proceeded to elect a successor whose name they sent on by their messengers to the King for approval, and the King in turn sent them on to Rome with his recommendation. The Pope's appointment was then sanctioned by the King, and the latter extorted from the elect the oath of fealty for his temporalities which were in the King's hands during the vacancy, and swept into the royal exchequer. Indeed, frequently the King delayed the licence to elect—it would seem purposely—in order to fill his coffers. There was no remedy against all this. No doubt occasionally the Popes did administer a sharp reminder to the English Kings in their attempt to interfere with the jurisdiction of ecclesiastical courts, but the other usurped royal privileges were down through the centuries recognised by the Holy See.

When Henry VIII came to the throne in 1509 there were four archbishoprics and twenty-eight suffragan bishoprics in Ireland. Between that year and 1547, the year of his death, there were about seventy-three appointments to Irish Sees. About forty-two of those appointments were made during the years previous to 1534, while Henry clung faithfully to his allegiance to the Holy See. It will be remembered that until Henry's failure to secure a divorce from Queen Catherine, the Holy See had no more devoted son than himself. He enjoyed all the privileges of a rich monarch in whose fidelity the Holy See placed implicit trust. It is not surprising that amongst the privileges handed down to him through a long line of Catholic ancestors, the power of presenting bishops to Irish Sees should have been one of the most important. It is not likely that he exercised this privilege with regard to all the Irish Sees, as some of them were outside the sphere of his authority and of his influence. But he certainly enjoyed it in the case of most of them. This will appear the more remarkable when it is borne in mind that during the entire period of Henry's fidelity to the Holy See, the Pale boundary, beyond which his English subjects did not dare to venture, and which protected them from the " Irish rebels," was confined to the four obedient shires. Dublin, Meath, Kildare, and Oriel (Louth) constituted the region of the King's civil influence as a ruler in Ireland.

It is worth while recording the bounds of the Pale in 1515. " The English Pale doth stretch and extend from the town of Dundalk to the town of Darver, to the town of Ardee, always on the left side, leaving the March [boundary] on the right, and so to the town of Siddan, to the town of Keels, to the town of Dangan, to Kilcock, to the town of Clane, to the town of Naas, to the Bridge of Kilcullen, to the town of Ballymore-Eustace and so backward to the town of Rathmore, and to the town of Rathcool, to the town of Tallaght, and to the town of Dalkey, leaving always the march on the right hand from the said Dundalk to the said town of Dalkey." Yet this region, by the year 1537, had been considerably diminished by the encroachments of the Irish clans, and the new line ran from Dundalk to Dunboyne, to Leixlip, Kildrought (Celbridge), Oughterard, Rathcoole, Saggart, Tallaght, and on to the walls of Dublin. Kilcock, Clane, Naas, Rathmore, Ballymore-Eustace, and the whole of South Co. Dublin had been removed from English control. Thus the Pale had dwindled into a district of not more than " twenty miles in compass." And yet Henry VIII writes to the Pope presenting bishops to sees as far distant from the Pale as Raphoe (1514), Clogher (1515), Clonmacnoise (1515), Ross (1517), Ardagh (1517).

There can be no doubt, therefore, that Henry enjoyed a real power over the Irish Church. His influence was recognised by Irish churchmen themselves, who had recourse to him to secure provisions to sees. It was recognised by the Holy See, which in the nine cases in which there is record of his request, appointed the candidate he named. It was by no means an advantageous circumstance that the influences of English Kings and English Churchmen thus interposed in the relations between the Irish Church and the Holy See. The efforts of England were directed to destroying all direct intercourse between Ireland and Rome. This was the meaning of the contempt hurled by John Alen [1] against the Irish " Rome runners," namely, in 1529, before Henry broke off relations with the Holy See. The man who was the instrument of this concentration of ecclesiastical power within the shores of England was Thomas Cardinal Wolsey, Papal Legate.

Thomas Wolsey, the son of a wealthy townsman of Ipswich, had risen to the post of Minister of Henry VIII. The new states-man reversed the policy of his predecessor ; he concentrated all authority in home and foreign affairs in his own hands. As Chancellor he stood at the head of public justice, and as Papal Legate he was supreme in the Church. As Chancellor, even More—his avowed enemy—confessed that he surpassed all men's expectation. The Court of Chancery became crowded with business through the character for expedition and justice which it acquired under his rule. His vast powers in Church and State made it incumbent upon the Cardinal to erect a court which had hitherto been unknown to the common law, called the Legatine Court, where matters of conscience were inquired into. It was this vast concentration of all secular and ecclesiastical power in a single hand which accus-tomed England to the personal government that began with Henry VIII. It was, above all, Wolsey's long tenure of the whole papal authority within the realm, and the consequent sus-pension of appeals to Rome, which led men to acquiesce at a later time in Henry's religious supremacy.[2] One of Wolsey's energetic and trusted officials, in legatine and chancery court, was John Alen. Alen was educated at Oxford,[3] where his brilliant abilities brought him under the notice of Warham, Archbishop of Canter-bury, who in 1515 entrusted him with important negotiations at

---

[1] A relative of John Alen, Archbishop of Dublin.

[2] Green, *Hist. of the English People*, p. 317.

[3] He afterwards went to Cambridge where he was made M.A., or, as some think, LL.B. (*Athen. Oxon.*, i. 35).

the Court of Rome. He remained there about nine years, and received the degree of LL.D., either there or in some university in Italy. The satisfaction he had given was sufficient introduction to Wolsey. By him he was appointed as a kind of overseer to Warham, Archbishop of Canterbury (18 March, 1519),[1] and a few years later (20 Oct., 1522)[2] he was evidently judge in Chancery, whilst in 1524 he was making out, in the Legatine Court, the pro-curations due to Wolsey from various places in and around London.[3] " In that office he was thought to be a perjured and wicked per-son."[4] In the latter end of 1525 he was incorporated LL.D. of Oxford.

Having appointed him his chaplain, Wolsey issued to Alen a commission to dissolve forty of the lesser monasteries for the endowment of the Cardinal's colleges at Oxford and Ipswich (1524).[5] At this time Dr. Alen was a canon of Lincoln. Soon he was appointed one of the ministers of the King's Chapel, and was employed in the re-examination of the Hanse merchants who were suspected of heresy. During the judicial proceedings in connec-tion with the King's divorce, 17 May, 1527, Alen was one of the law doctors who were present as *testes*, and in the list of members of Wolsey's suite he is mentioned as one of the two *audiencers*.[6] In fact, Alen's presence seems to have become indispensable to Wolsey. He was in France with him, 27 July, 1527, and Wolsey, in a letter to the King from Amiens, says he is sending Dr. Alen to him to learn his pleasure and receive his instructions in regard to State affairs.

[1] *L. and P. Hen. VIII*, vol. iii., Part I.   [2] *Ib.*, vol. iii., Part II.
[3] *Ib.*, vol. iv., Part I.   [4] *Athen. Oxon.*, i. 35.
[5] *L. and P. Hen. VIII*, vol. iv., Part I. Alen incurred great odium for his part in this transaction. Roy's satire against Wolsey shows this :—

    Wat.   And who did for the show pay ?
    Jeff.   Truly many a rich abbaye
            To be eased of his visitation.
    Wat.   Doth he in his own person visit ?
            No, another for him doth it,
            That can skill of the occupation.
            A fellow neither wise nor sad,
            But he was never yet full mad,
            Though he be frantic and more.
            Dr. Alen he is named,
            One that to lie is not ashamed
            If he spy advantage therefore.
    Wat.   Are such with him in any price ?
    Jeff.   Yea, for they do all his advice,
            Whether it be wrong or right.
                  (*Harleian Miscellany*, vol. ix.)
[6] *L. and P. Hen. VIII*, vol. iv., Part II.

As a reward for his services Alen was selected by the King, and evidently through the influence of Wolsey, for the See of Dublin. There is no indication that the usual election was held on this occasion, but Henry supplicated the Holy See to have Alen appointed. It would seem that the King did not wait for the papal appointment, but sent Alen at once to Dublin. Hugh Inge, Alen's predecessor in the see, had died on 3 August, 1528, and though Alen had been appointed about November of that year to go to Rome on State affairs, yet this arrangement was cancelled, and Alen was despatched to Dublin " with great speed." He waited from Christmas until Candlemas (1529) at Chester for a favourable wind, and evidently reached Dublin in February. But he had to wait until 3 September (1529) for the papal Bulls, and on the 10th of that month a mandate was issued that the pallium should be conferred.[1] When he was consecrated is a matter of some difficulty, but it would appear to have been on the second Sunday in Lent, 1530, and evidently in Christ Church.[2] Besides being appointed archbishop, Alen was made Chancellor of Ireland, and also vice-legate in Ireland of Cardinal Wolsey.[3]

The extraordinary haste in the sending of Alen to Dublin is explained by the hatred of Wolsey for Gerald, Earl of Kildare, " whom his Eminence by many plots and snares endeavoured to pull down." [4] Alen was a pugnacious individual, and evidently the strong man to deal with the extraordinary power over the country wielded by the Kildares. We shall see the result of this feud between the Alens and Butler (Earl of Ossory) on one side and the Fitzgeralds on the other.

A few incidents during Alen's administration of the see call for observation, as they indicate a leading up to the events of Browne's reign. One of these was concerned with the granting of faculties and dispensations, a second with Henry's treatment of Alen, and a third was contained in the Geraldine revolt. As to the first, it is useful to state that on the return of Cardinal Campeggio to Rome (he had been joint legate with Wolsey), Leo X granted to Wolsey alone, by Bull dated 6 January, 1520,[5] all the powers that

[1] Brady, *Episcopal Succession*, i. 326.

[2] Ware's *Bishops* (346) gives Christ Church as the place of consecration and 13 March, 1528 (*English style*, i.e. 1529) as the date. *Athen. Oxon.* also gives 1528 (*same style*). The *Liber Albus*, Christ Church (*Cal.* by Dr. Lawler, p. 14), gives second Sunday in Lent, 1529, which the editor makes equivalent to 1530.

[3] In 1531 a suffragan or coadjutor bishop was appointed to assist Alen. This was Richard Gama, a Franciscan, under the title of Bishop of Tiberiadis.

[4] Ware, *loc. cit.*   [5] Rymer's *Fœdera*, xiii, 734.

had been enjoyed by himself and Campeggio. And Wolsey appointed Alen, on provision to Dublin, his vice-legate in Ireland. Now, in the Bull of Leo there is no mention of Ireland, but only of the Kingdom of England and its provinces.[1] Grave doubt arose among the Irish bishops and clergy as to whether Wolsey was legate in Ireland. Consequently, instead of applying to Alen for the dispensations, they applied to Rome. At this time one of the Archbishop's relatives, another John Alen, had been appointed to the clerkship of the Council in Ireland by Wolsey, through the Archbishop's influence, and to report to the Cardinal on the state of the country. This John Alen wrote a letter (1 June, 1529) to Wolsey on the question of the legatine jurisdiction, which it is well to give in its entirety :—[2]

Pleaseth it your honourable Grace to pardon me of my presumption in writing to the same, thinking it my duty, for that ye have whichsaved [vouchsafed] to admit me (much unworthily) to your service, to ascertain your Grace, from time to time, of the causes committed to me. Herein enclosed your Grace shall receive such a scrow of dispensations and other things, as hath been sped by your honourable authority, since our coming to these exile parts, containing what sums of money have and shall be received for the same. Assuring your Grace, it is great marvel that so much is done, considering the unseen poverty that is in the Englishry, at this season, otherwise than hitherto it hath been, as it is said, and thine establishment of the same : so that we have no resort to us, aught of the Irishry, for any of your faculties. And although alway messengers hitherto might pass safely, yet now many times they been robbed and spoiled or murdered.

Over this, if my Lord of Dublin were not the King's Chancellor, whereby he doth punish, with temporal power,[3] such as would resist your authority, it were not likely to be executed here with so much

---

[1] The Bull is addressed : " Leo episcopus, etc., dilecto filio Thomae Titulo Sanctae Ceciliae Presbytero Cardinali in Regno Angliae nostro et apostolicae Sedis legato." It concludes : " seculares ecclesiasticas personas ac clerum regni et provinciarum hujusmodi."

[2] *L. and P. Hen. VIII*, vol. iv., Part III, p. 2488. A similar letter is given in *State Papers, Hen. VIII*, iii. 102, dated 1 June, 1523-24. There is some mistake about the latter date. There is nothing to show when Alen was made clerk of the Council. But when he wrote the letter, " my Lord of Dublin," i.e. the Archbishop, was " the King's Chancellor." Now this must refer to Archbishop Alen. It does not refer to his predecessor Inge, who was not appointed Chancellor until 1527. Consequently, the letter refers to the state of affairs which confronted Archbishop Alen shortly after his arrival in Dublin, and to the doubt about his own office of vice-legate. The letter above is given from the *State Papers, Hen. VIII*, iii. 102, 1523-24, as the *Letters and Papers, Hen. VIII ad an.* 1529, only give a calendar of it.

[3] Namely, in virtue of his temporal jurisdiction in his manor courts.

*b**

honour, as it is ; for much doubt is made about your Grace's Bulls, whether ye be Legate here or not ; insomuch we be in fear to show the transsumptis [transcripts] of them, and besides that, we have neither [a]bridgements nor transumptes, according to your Grace's commandment. Beseeching the same, that I may have the transumptes of all your Bulls, from the day of your first creation Legate. For your Grace hath some faculties that ye use not ; whereof one is, after deprivation, by your Grace made, of an abbot or prior, etc., from their dignity, ye may make provision of the same, notwithstanding election. This was granted to Laurence [1] and your Grace jointly ; yet Leo hath innovate, and confirmed it to your Grace, in such wise, as though it had been granted to you alone. About the degrees of consanguinity and affinity, your Grace's Bulls be not very clear for this country, which hurteth. Wherefore herein enclosed I do send your Grace a copy of a Bull of this Pope, granted heretofore to the collector, which Raphael Maruff did use in Ireland, wherein the doubts, that I moved to your Grace about the same, ye shall mowe [more] see right well declared ; trusting your Grace will have yours, after the same wise.

Besides this, my Lord Chancellor is very difficile in granting of your dispensations (which hindreth your Grace), and is less to be regarded in this land than anywhere. For many parts under the King's obeisance there been penal statutes, that no Englishman shall marry with the Irish, so that they be so intricate in consanguinity or affinity, and besides that, the people of themselves be so propine to evil, they would marry without dispensation, unless be enforced to sue to the Court of Rome. Whereof hath ensued the decay of the Church of Ireland ; for, when an idle person [i.e. gentleman] goeth to the Court of Rome, the compositions be to Irishmen so small for their poverty, that by him many other exorbitant matters be sped. So that, in this land, your Grace's dispensations be necessary to be granted with less difficulty, than elsewhere, for the avoiding of contempt of holy canons, and the occasion of the inconvenience that followeth of these Rome runners. And over that, that the manner of the compositions in this land, for their poverty, should be reduced from sterling money to the money of this country ; whereby I suppose we should speed three dispensations than to one now.

Finally, may it please your noble Grace to remember us, that to do your Grace service, been returned from our own, living as it were in captivity, in great fear daily of our enemies. Insomuch the Chief Justice showeth me, that if English power cometh not shortly, we shall fain to return from hence at Michaelmas. And I (by the Deputy and Council's indifferent [impartial] election) occupying (unworthy) the clerkship of the Council, do perceive and know the patched and unhonourable truces, which, by enforcement of pure necessity, be tolerated. Whereby I do perceive how much England

---

[1] Cardinal Campeggio.

is bound to pray for your Grace, who peradventure sometime should know part of Ireland's misery, were not your Grace's high and excellent wisdom, experience, and noble justice. That knoweth God, who ever preserve your noble Grace in long life, with continuance in honour. From Dublin, the first of June.

Your Grace's most humble servant and Register.

(Signed) JOHN ALEN.

[*Superscribed.*]

Reverendissimo in Christo Patri, ac Domino, Domino, Thome, tituli Sancte Cecilie Presbytero Cardinali, Apostolicae Sedis in Anglia et Hibernia de Latere Legato, Domino meo colendissimo.

A brief commentary will be useful on this letter. The Irish did not resort to Archbishop Alen for the dispensations, and it was only his temporal power that secured compliance in the Pale. It was cheaper to apply to Rome, when one messenger could secure a number of dispensations. It is important to emphasise this point in view of the accusations made later on as to the excessive papal demands in such cases. But as to Wolsey's jurisdiction as legate in Ireland, even Archbishop Alen doubted, and was reluctant to grant the dispensations. He was held in little esteem by the Irish, as he was Wolsey's friend and agent. Alen, the clerk of the Council, seems also to have had some doubt as to the jurisdiction, and remarked how strange it was that no transcript of Wolsey's legatine Bulls had been sent to the Irish Chancery, and that this was according to the Cardinal's command. Henry and Wolsey had taken all power, ecclesiastical as well as civil, into their own hands, and Wolsey considered that he and the King had as much jurisdiction in Church and State over Ireland as over England. It was a dangerous move on the part of Wolsey, and made the King familiar with the Absolutism that he afterwards developed. While Wolsey was in power all was well, but, when he fell, Henry took the reins of Church and State into his own hands. We have already referred to the term " Rome runners " which Alen, the clerk, applied in contempt to those who sought the dispensations from Rome. It is significant, as it shows a certain antipathy to the papal court, and the term was afterwards applied very generally to those who did not agree with Henry's usurpation of ecclesiastical power. Lastly, so far as we can discover, Alen, the clerk, had no authority for inserting in his superscription to his letter the word *Hibernia* (Ireland) as signifying the extent of the Cardinal's legateship. Pope Leo's Bull simply mentions him as legate of the "kingdom of England." The Irish bishops and priests were doubtless aware of this, and resented the interference

of the English Cardinal and his agents in the ecclesiastical administration of Ireland.

That the King was fast developing Absolutism is shown in his
treatment of Archbishop Alen. Favours had been showered by the
Cardinal on the Archbishop, and the latter, like the former, was
to be the object of royal anger. Wolsey, who detested Anne Boleyn,
was, through her influence, removed from office, and surrendered
the Great Seal on 17 October, 1529. Henry, having drifted from
Rome, and finding that the clergy were his most strenuous opponents in the matter of divorce, determined to humble them.   In
December, 1530, the whole English nation was declared to be under
premunire in having acquiesced in Wolsey's legatine authority.[1]
The clergy were told that the King was willing " upon a reasonable
composition and a full submission to pardon them." Alen did
not escape the penalty for having been Wolsey's commissary and
vice-legate.   He was commanded by Henry to yield his archbishopric into the King's hands, and he made a formal profession [2]
(4 Feb., 1531) that he held his " archbishopric and all its manors
and emoluments " of the Crown. He did not receive a general
pardon or the release of his possessions until 7 February, 1532.[3]
For his offence against *premunire* he was fined £1466 13s. 4d.[4]
During the period of his suspension he had evidently appointed
to benefices in his diocese, for he was again fined for his " second
great *premunire*." [5]

Moreover, Cromwell advised Henry that the revenues of the
archbishopric should be called for to the King's use, and that the
first fruits of the see were to be employed on the building of the
castles of Wicklow, Arklow, Green Castle, Powerscourt, Newcastle
McKynegan, Castlekevin, Castellankelly, and Ballymore. Some of
these were the Archbishop's manors, on the borders of the Pale.
Considering that Alen had not received his chancellor's fee, and
that he had spent his own money in putting the Chancery in Dublin
Castle, which was " more like a swine-sty," into decent condition,
and in refurnishing ships and hostings for the King, he was badly
rewarded by Henry. This was not all. In the articles for the

[1] Hore, *Hist. of Church of England*. " Wolsey, by acting as the Pope's
legate *a latere*, had broken the law of the land, and had incurred the penalty of
premunire. But it was a flagrant act of injustice on the part of the King to en-
force it against him. Henry had himself obtained the post for him, had granted
him under the Great Seal his license to hold it, and he had allowed him to perform its duties for many years."

[2] *L. and P. Hen. VIII*, vol. v., no. 657.

[3] *Ib.*, no. 779. Rymer, xiv. 430.

[4] About £22,000, according to *1914 value*, or about fifteen times that value.

[5] Letter to Cromwell, 19 March, 1532. *L. P. Hen. VIII*, vol. v., no. 412.

government of Ireland (1534) it was " ordained by the King and his most honourable council that the lands of the spirituality and benefices to all common charges of the country shall contribute as the lands of the temporality are charged, and all lords and other persons of the spirituality shall send companies to hostings and journeys in manner and form following : the Archbishop of Armagh 16 able archers or gunners, appointed for war ; the Archbishop of Dublin, 20 ditto, etc." These were new burdens imposed on prelates to assist the spendthrift King.

An incident that cannot be passed over as having some influence on the course of events during the " reform " period is the deadly feud that arose between the Alens and the Butlers on the one side, and the Kildares on the other. It helped, so to speak, to stiffen the backs of the Irish against the Absolutism of Henry. Wolsey had been the implacable enemy of the Kildares, and had had Archbishop Alen appointed Chancellor to counteract the enormous influence of Earl Gerald. Gerald, as deputy, had dismissed the Archbishop from the chancellorship, and had given it to Cromer, Archbishop of Armagh. The Alens, relatives of Archbishop Alen, joined with the Butlers of Ossory in bringing about the downfall of Gerald. And, it is said, that the Archbishop and John Alen, Master of the Rolls, were mainly instrumental in spreading the false rumour that Gerald had been beheaded, and in thus goading on the impetuous Silken Thomas, Gerald's son, into revolt. But they did not reckon on the Geraldine preparations. Fearful of his own safety, the Archbishop took ship from Damme's Gate near Dublin Castle, but pursued and caught at Howth by Thomas's men, he was brought to Artane, where he was murdered and quartered before Thomas's eyes. Alen, like Wolsey, had suffered in his devotion to the cause of an ungrateful King.

But the revolt now takes a new turn. According to Chapuys, ambassador of Charles V at London, Silken Thomas had a following of 20,000 men, and was demanding the loyalty of the Irish towns, and this, he says, was done " in order that he may show his Holiness that all is done in behalf of the faith and the Holy See." This was on 11 August, 1534. In another letter (29 Aug.) he says that those of the towns where he has entered have sworn fealty to the Pope, to the Emperor, and to himself.[1] The introduction of the Pope into this revolt against the King of England shows the class of opposition that was being prepared in Ireland against Henry. In 1533 Henry had married Anne Boleyn, and in March of the following year he was threatened by the Pope with excommunication.

[1] *L. and P. Hen. VIII*, vol. vii.

Thus the rupture between Rome and England was complete, and the Convocations of Canterbury and York declared that " the Pope has no greater jurisdiction conferred on him by God in Holy Scriptures in the Kingdom of England than any other foreign bishop." Such was the state of affairs when Chapuys wrote those letters, and when Silken Thomas was demanding the fealty of the Irish towns for the Pope, and opposition to the King on religious grounds.

It will be useful to state now some of the accusations brought against the Church in Ireland at this period. Inge, Archbishop of Dublin, wrote (23 Feb., 1528) to Wolsey : " Your Grace, we doubt not, heareth the sorrowful decay of this land, as well in good Christianity, as other laudable manners : which hath grown for lack of good prelates and curates in the Church. Wherefore, your Grace may do meritoriously, to see such persons promoted to bishopricks that their manner of living may be example of goodness and virtue. The residence of such shall do more good than we can express." Inge, being an Englishman, like his predecessors in the see since the Anglo-Norman occupation, did not look with favour on Irishmen as prelates or as the occupants of vicarages among his own countrymen in Ireland. It can scarcely be presumed that he had much acquaintance with the Church in the Irish parts. As a matter of fact, his chief grievance in his letter was relative to the diocese of Meath, which had no bishop at the time.

The question of papal provisions to sees and benefices was another reason put forth for the decay in the Church. In England these provisions of foreigners to benefices had estranged the nobility in a great measure in their loyalty to the Holy See, as they thus deprived the lords of patronage to benefices and their sons of easy and lucrative livings. In Ireland a similar outcry took place. The Earl of Kildare, in 1525, declared that the churches in Tipperary and Kilkenny were generally in ruins through the system, " so as, and if the King's Grace do not see for the hasty remedy of the same, there is like to be no more Christianity there, than in the midst of Turkey." [1] The Earl was not impartial. He had the patronage of a vast amount of rectories, and probably had his eyes fixed on others. The King was just beginning to quarrel with the Pope, and evidently the Earl considered that Henry would be ready enough to believe that papal provisions had ruined the churches.

A more serious indictment was that made by Sir Peter Butler,

[1] *S.P. Hen. VIII*, vol. ii., p. 123.

Earl of Ossory, the sworn enemy of the Geraldines in their revolt against the King, and one of the leaders of the " reform " under Henry. In an indenture of 31 May, 1534, he declares :—[1]

The Bishop of Rome's provisions and usurped jurisdiction have been the chief cause of the desolation and decay of Ireland, " by the abominable abuse whereof the cathedral churches, in monasteries, parish churches, and all other regular and secular, for the more part, in effect through the land, been in utter ruin and destroyed : for the said Bishop of Rome commonly hath preferred by his provisions to the administration and governance of them not only vile and vicious persons unlearned, being murderers, thieves, and of other detestable disposition, as light men of war, who, for their unjust maintenance therein for some time to expel the rightful incumbent, and other seasons by force of secular power to put the true patrons from their patronage, and other their misorders, have not only spent, wasted, and alienate such lands as the King, his noble progenitors, and his nobles gave to the augmentation of God's divine service in the churches of that land, the exhibition and maintenance of the ministers of the same, and the utensils and ornaments there, but also by occasion of the same great wars hath been stirred amongst the King's people and countries virent [sic],[2] bishops and divers other persons spiritual and temporal murdered, and many other detestable things have ensued thereby." Therefore the King has willed his deputy to resist with all his power the abuse and usurped jurisdiction of the said Bishop of Rome ; and the Earl of Ossory has promised that he and his son will resist the said provisions with all their power.

Such of the Irish or English as shall be brought to good conformity by means of the said Earl and his son shall be favourably accepted, entertained, and aided by the Deputy and Council.

The Earl of Ossory had promised that he and his son, Lord James Butler, would assist the Deputy against the King's Irish and English rebels.

We cannot accept Butler as an impartial witness. He had already thrown in his lot with Henry against the Geraldine revolt and all it implied, and against the jurisdiction of the Pope in Ireland. He already rules himself out as an impartial witness when he declares that he is ready to resist the " usurped jurisdiction of the said Bishop of Rome." He had evidently been influenced by the progress of events in ecclesiastical affairs in England, and was preparing the way for the King's supremacy in Ireland. But we have the testimony of Henry's own words to rebut the allegation that the papal power exercised in provisions to Irish benefices had brought the Irish Church to a state of utter ruin and left it in

---

[1] *Car. Cal. S.P.I.*, pp. 54-5. [2] *Videlicet* (?)

need of reform. We have his own words upon the qualifications of the priests whom he recommended to the Holy See for provision to Irish dioceses and the testimonies elicited by the secretaries of the Pope. Henry's recommendation and eulogy were not accepted by the Pope without careful scrutiny ; they were usually referred for inquiry. An examination of the various recommendations will show that these priests were learned, fit to govern, especially modest, of irreproachable morals, some of them of great sanctity and learning. The Pope provided neither ignorant nor unlearned, nor carelessly living prelates. It is only what we should expect.

The power of the bishop over his clergy and his churches was different in some important respects from the system obtaining to-day in Ireland. Just as the monarch stood between the Irish Episcopate and the Pope, laymen and the priors of the monasteries stood between the bishop and a great proportion of his clergy.[1] The monasteries owned an enormously large number of the parish churches, and their priors exercised the patronage of them. In the list that we give of the possessions of the religious houses of the diocese of Dublin we see the large number of rectories owned by those houses all over the country. An extent of all the religious houses of Ireland would reveal an extraordinary situation in the Irish Church. No doubt this was the growth of centuries, and these possessions and their accompanying rights of advowson or patronage were largely the gifts of pious laymen. But besides this there remained churches over which laymen continued to retain control, and while the confirmation of lay appointments belonged of right to the bishop, the clergy of such churches owed their livings to the laymen's gift, and a corresponding sense of dependence upon lay liberality was bred in them from which, when the interests of religion are considered, it would have been better they had been free. The cataclysm of the " Reformation " destroyed in the Catholic Church all these bonds of lay dependency. The Protestant Church that fell into the temporal inheritance of the Irish Church inherited also this legacy of lay control.

Neither can it be said that absenteeism on the part of bishops or beneficiaries brought decay on the Irish Church. Absenteeism amongst the bishops was an abuse that in England was attended with serious consequences to the discipline of the clergy and the spiritual care of the subject. The evidences of the presence of this abuse in the Irish Church are not frequent, but they apply, as far as can be ascertained, only to the English occupants of Irish

---

[1] It may be interesting to note that in the year 1531 Archbishop Alen had " about 40 collative livings in right of the Church of Dublin belonging unto him " (*Loftus MSS., ad an.*).

sees. No such complaints have been recorded, as far as we can discover, against Irishmen.

Lastly, it cannot be said that wealth was a source of corruption in the Irish Church. In earthly possessions the great majority of the Irish bishops could not be called wealthy. Compared with their English brethren, many of them were poor indeed. The Earl of Kildare replied, on a famous occasion, to a taunt of Cardinal Wolsey, that if he exchanged kingdoms with the Cardinal he would guarantee to gather up more crumbs in one month than twice the revenues of his poor earldom. If we take the papal taxation of sees as a fair basis of comparison we shall find that in this period the normal taxable capacity of all the Irish dioceses taken together was not equal to the sum levied against the opulent incumbent of the single English diocese of Winchester. Winchester was taxed at 12,000 gold florins,[1] whilst the taxation of the thirty-two dioceses of Ireland only reached 11,837.[2] Dublin and Cashel provided more than half of that sum, and Armagh and Meath more than a quarter. So that the remaining twenty-eight dioceses only contributed a paltry quarter. Yet we must admit a difficulty in accepting papal taxation as a satisfactory basis of comparison. If in the papal list the taxation figures imposed bore a uniform proportion to the revenues, it would be possible to form some estimate of the annual income of the Irish bishops in the smaller and poorer sees. But the figures show that no uniform standard was observed. On the other hand, if we take the valuation of some of the Irish Sees according to extents made in 1537-8-9,[3] we find that many of the bishops were far from poor. And in the figures given no account is taken, presumably, of the incidental revenues of the bishops. The following list will be of interest :—

Diocese.	Irish Money.	Sterling.	1914 value.
Armagh . . .	£183 17 5½	£137 18 0¾	£2070
Meath . . .	—	373 12 0	5610
Dublin . . .	534 15 2½	401 1 4½	6015
Kildare . . .	69 11 4	52 3 6	780
Ossory . . .	100 marks =	66 13 4	990
Ferns . . .	108 13 4	81 10 0	1215
Cashel . . .	66 13 4	50 0 0	750
Waterford and Lismore	72 8 1	54 6 0¾	810

From all this the general conclusion may be drawn that a great

[1] John Alen, Archbishop of Dublin, paid 2650 gold florins for his bulls.
[2] See Gogarty, *Ir. Theol. Quart.*, Oct., 1912.
[3] Harris, *Ware's Bishops*, at head of each diocese.

number of the Irish bishops enjoyed no more than a mere com-
petence. And if we may argue from the financial condition of the
Irish Episcopate in Henry's reign, we may also conclude that the
Irish Church did not suffer from the evil influences to which a
ponderously wealthy Church might be said to have fallen a prey.

In raising Wolsey to be head of Church and State, Henry, as
we have seen, had simply gathered all religious as well as all civil
authority into his personal grasp. The nation that trembled
before Wolsey learned to tremble before the King, who had
destroyed Wolsey with a breath. And now Thomas Cromwell, the
" most terrible figure in our history " and the prince of opportunists,
appears on the stage. It is difficult to get at an accurate estimate
of the nature of Cromwell's first dealings with Henry. We know
he gained the ear of his sovereign, and that within a comparatively
short time after Wolsey's death Cromwell was Henry's most
trusted adviser. "We know that the concerted attack on the
Church sprang out of some suggestion of Cromwell's, but we do
not know the exact nature of the suggestion." [1] Money seems to
have been at the back of it all. " By 1530," continues the same
writer, " perhaps long before, Henry, most extravagant of English
sovereigns, had not only got through the millions left to him by
his thrifty father—Stubbs credits Henry VII with having left
£1,800,000—but also through the liberal supplies extorted at
various times from commons and clergy by Warham, Wolsey, and
More. About 1530 he was, in my opinion, at his wit's end for
money : I believe he turned to Cromwell, a smart and crafty
business man, for financial advice ; I believe that Cromwell coolly
pointed to the Church." The advice struck the keynote of the
later policy by which the daring counsellor was to change the
whole face of Church and State. Such was the state of affairs
when a successor was appointed in Dublin to Archbishop Alen—
unrest and dissatisfaction not only among the Irish but among the
Anglo-Norman lords. A new element had been introduced into
the conflict between England and Ireland—opposition to Henry
on religious grounds. It was still a slender flame, but the appointment of George Browne to the See of Dublin, without any appeal
to, or approval from, the Pope, fanned the flame and opened up a
new era in the history of the Anglo-Norman colony of Dublin.

[1] J. S. Fletcher, *The Reformation in Northern England*, p. 22.

BIBLIOGRAPHY.

Account Roll, Christ Church, *ed*. Mills.
Additional MSS., British Museum, 4789.
Alen, Archbishop, Register (Liber Niger), MS.
Alen, Archbishop, Repertorium Viride MS.
Archdall, Monasticon Hibernicon.
Archivium Hibernicum (Rev. T. Gogarty on Primate Dowdall).
Athenæ Oxonienses.
Athenæum, 1886.

Bagwell, Ireland under the Tudors.
Bale, John, Vocacyon (Harleian Miscellany, vol. vi.).
Bernard, St. Patrick's Cathedral.
Book of Common Prayer, 1551, T.C.D.
Book of Lismore.
Bracton, De Legibus et Consuetudinibus Angliæ.
Brady, Episcopal Succession.
Bridgett, Rev. T. E., Blunders and Forgeries.
Burnet, Historical Records.

Calendar, Ancient Records of Dublin, *ed*. Gilbert.
Calendar, Documents of Ireland, *ed*. Sweetman.
Calendar, Patent Rolls, Edward VI.
Calendar, Letters and Papers, Henry VIII.
Calendar, Patent and Close Rolls, Ireland, Henry VIII, Edward and
    Mary.
Calendar, State Papers, Henry VIII, Ireland.
Calendar, State Papers, Ireland (Carew).
Chalmers, National Biography.
Chancery Inquisitions.
Chancery Rolls.
Chartularies, St. Mary's Abbey, *ed*. Gilbert.
Christ Church Deeds, D.K.R.I. Reports.
Cobbett, Protestant Reformation, Part 2.
Constant, Le transformation du culte anglicain sous Edouard VI.
Cooper, Austin, Diary.
Cottonian MSS., British Museum.

Cox, Hibernia Anglicana.
Crede Mihi, *ed.* Gilbert.

De Burgo, Hibernia Dominicana.
Dignitas Decani, Cal. *ed.* Bernard (R.I.A.).
Dowdall, Register.
Dowling, Annals, I.A.A.
Dublin Corporation, Archives, All Hallows Box.

English Historical Review, 1895.
Erasmus, Opera Ambrosii, T.C.D., 1538.
Extent, Religious Houses, Diocese of Dublin, *Unpublished MS.*,
    P.R.O., London.

Fiants, D.K.R.I. Reports.
Fletcher, Reformation in Northern England.
Four Masters, Annals of Ireland.

Gairdner, Church of England.
Gairdner, Lollardy and the Reformation.
Gasquet, Card., Eve of the Reformation.
Gasquet, Card., Henry VIII and English Monasteries.
Gasquet and Bishop, Edward VI and the Book of Common Prayer.
Gihr, Holy Sacrifice of the Mass.
Gilbert, History of Dublin.
Graves, Presentment of Grievances.
Green, History of the English People.
Grose, Antiquities of Ireland.

Halliday, Scandinavian Dublin.
Harleian Miscellany, Life of Abp. Browne, vol. v.
Harris, Hibernica.
Harris, MSS. R.D.S. Library.
Harris, Ware's Bishops.
Hogan, Hibernia Ignatiana.
Hogan, Onomasticon Hibernicon.
Hollingshed, Chronicles.

Irish Ecclesiastical Record, 1925.
Irish Statutes.
Irish Theological Quarterly, 1912, 1913, 1914.

Joyce, Irish Names of Places.

Kildare, Archæological Society, Publications.
Kilkenny, Archæological Society, Publications.
King, *Collectanea MS.* (National Library, Dublin).

Lambeth Palace Library, MSS.
Lawlor, Chapel of Dublin Castle (*R.S.A.I.*).
Leland, History of Ireland.
Lewis, Topographical Dictionary.
Liber Albus and Liber Niger, *Cal. ed.* Lawlor.
Lingard, History of England.
Lodge, Peerages.
Loftus MSS., Marsh's Library, Dublin.
Lynch, De Presulibus Hiberniæ.

MacNeill, Chas., Monastery Rolls (R.S.A.I.).
MacNeill, Chas., St. John's Hospital, Newgate (R.S.A.I.).
MacNeill, Chas., Hospitallers, Kilmainham (R.S.A.I.).
Mant, Church History of Ireland.
Martyrology of Donegal.
Martyrology of St. Thomas's Abbey, MS., T.C.D.
Mason, St. Patrick's Cathedral.
McInerny, History of Irish Dominicans.
Merriman, Life and Letters of Thomas Cromwell.
Müller, Die Bekenntnisschriften der reformierten Kirche.

Novum Registrum, Christ Church.

Obits and Martyrology, Christ Church, *ed.* Crosthwaite.
O'Donovan, History of Nannius.
Ordinance Survey Office, Co. Kildare Letters.

Pastor, Lives of the Popes, vol. xiii.
Pembridge, Annals.
Pipe Rolls.
Pococke, Richard, Diary through Ireland.

Records of Ireland, Deputy Keeper Reports.
Red Book, Privy Council of Ireland.
Register, All Hallows, *ed.* Butler.
Register, Archbishop Alen (Liber Niger), MS.
Register, Primate Dowdall, MS., T.C.D.
Register, St. John's Hospital, Newgate, MS.
Register, St. Thomas's Abbey, *ed.* Gilbert.
Ronan, Ancient Chapel Royal (I.E.R., 1923).
Ronan, Booke out of Irlande (I.E.R., 1925).
Ronan, Dublin Medieval Gilds (I.E.R., 1925).
Royal Irish Academy, Proceedings and Transactions.
Royal Society of Antiquaries of Ireland, Publications.
Rymer, Fœdera.

Shirley, Original Letters on Church in Ireland.
Spicilegium Ossoriense, *ed.* Moran.

State Papers, Henry VIII. (published).
State Papers, Henry VIII., P.R.O., London (unpublished).
Strype, Life of Cranmer.
Strype, Life of Parker.
Strype, Memorials Ecclesiastical.
Stubb's Register.

Theiner, Vetera Monumenta Hib. et. Scot.
Trinity College, Dublin, MSS., various.

Wadding, Annals.
Ware, Annals.
Ware (Robert), Life of Archbishop Browne (Harleian Miscellany, vol. v.).
Whitney, The Reformation.

PART I.

EVE OF THE "REFORMATION."

BROWNE, AN ENGLISH AUGUSTINIAN FRIAR.

NOTHING seems to be known about the parents of George Browne or about the place or year of his birth. It is said that he received his early education in the house of the Augustinian Order near Holywell in Oxfordshire, where Wadham College now stands.[1] Whether he entered the Order in that house or elsewhere does not appear. The earliest date mentioned in connection with him is the year 1523 when, it is said, he appealed for the degree of bachelor of divinity, but it does not appear that he was then admitted to that degree.[2] According to the regulations obtaining in theological schools of the period it was necessary for a student to apply himself diligently to his studies for five years before obtaining the degree of bachelor. It would seem then that in 1523 Browne had already studied for the five years, and, as he could scarcely have been less than eighteen years of age when he began his theology, the year of his birth would have been about 1500. No reason has been assigned for Browne's failure to obtain the coveted degree.

The next occasion on which he appears is in connection with a business transaction with Thomas Cromwell,[3] the power

[1] *Harleian Miscellany*, v. 595, note. According to the *Athenae Oxonienses* (i. 678) he "was educated in Academicals among those of his Order in *Oxon.*," Oxford.

[2] *Athen. Oxon.*, l.c. The applying for the degree was termed the "Reading of the Sentences" (Scholastic.)

[3] Fletcher (*op. cit.*, p. 27-8), the latest writer on the Reformation period, says of Cromwell: "Cromwell was a nobody to start with—the son of a drunken, law-breaking ale-seller at Wimbledon (others make him the son of a blacksmith at Putney). He himself lived an adventurous, and, by his own confession, an ill-behaved life in his younger days. There is a good deal of mystery about those days; he is said to have been a soldier in Italy; certainly he was well acquainted with the Italian qualities of craft, cunning, and subtlety, and with

I

behind the throne. Cromwell, in 1532, had succeeded to
the responsible position of Master of the King's Jewels, and
Browne was prior of the Austin Friars at their celebrated
house in Thockmorton Street, London. For some reason
Cromwell wished to have two messuages or tenements adjoining Austin Friars and belonging to the Order, and an
indenture was drawn up (16 May, 1532) between William
Whetherall, provincial of the Order, and George Browne,
prior of Austin Friars in London, of the one part, and Thomas
Cromwell, master of the jewels, on the other, granting to the
latter a lease of ninety-nine years of two messuages,

" late of new builded, the fore front whereof abutteth upon the
west end of the wall of the churchyard there where the pulpit
now standeth "; with two gardens and a great warehouse belonging to one of the messuages late in the holding of John Cavalcanti.
These messuages lie " within the precinct or close of the said house
of Friars, abutting upon the lane there leading to the said Friars
church on the east partie, and upon the lands pertaining to the
heirs of John Braymounde of the west partie," and the lands of
the said Friars north and south. Also the tenement called the
Swanne, and the alley called Swanne Alley the end of which abuts
on the garden belonging to that one of the said two messuages in
which Cromwell now dwells on the north side, the other end abutting on the King's high street called Lothebury on the south;
one side of the said alley abutting on the said warehouse on the
east, and the other on the lands and tenements belonging to the
heirs of the said John Braymound on the west. In one of the said
two messuages, now in the tenure of Cromwell, John Cavalcanti,
merchant of Florence, lately dwelt.[1]

From this transaction it would seem that Cromwell,
while master of the jewels, was taking over the banking
establishment of the Florence merchant with the intention

the principles of Machiavelli. But wherever he spent his young-man time, he
was back in England, and practising as a solicitor in London, about the year
1512. Eight years later he appears to have attracted the notice of Wolsey, and
he was certainly employed by Wolsey in one capacity or another up to the time
of Wolsey's first fall. Wolsey's disappearance from the chief centre of things
signalizes Cromwell's entrance into it. For several years he was Henry's right-
hand man, much as Henry seems to have despised him. And during those
years, and especially while he was actively engaged in suppressing the religious
orders, Cromwell did very well for himself."

[1] L. and P. Hen. VIII, 1532, no. 1028.

of carrying on that business. But a more important inference may be drawn. It would seem to have been the beginning of the great friendship between Cromwell and Browne, which, growing stronger with the years, bound those two men together to carry out the behests of their royal master in his religious " reform." Browne, anxious for favours, or beset with difficulties, always threw himself on the friendship and at the mercy of Cromwell, appealing to him as to his " powerful right hand."

Six months later (October, 1532), licence was granted to George Browne, prior of the Augustine friars in London, among other friars, to go beyond the sea. There is nothing to point out the reason of this journey or the place to which he travelled. It may have been that he wished to attend a General Chapter of the Order or to take his degree in some foreign university.[1] But the journey seems to have been an eventful one for him. It is probable that, during this sojourn abroad, he became acquainted with the writings of Luther, and was influenced by the doctrine of the " reformers " which directed that prayers and petitions should be made solely and directly to Christ.[2]

HENRY VIII's SECOND MARRIAGE ; BROWNE'S ASSISTANCE.

Browne's stay abroad was of short duration as he was back in London in January, 1533. In the month of April (13th) he preached in London, and at once ranged himself on the side of the King against the Pope. Chapuys, the ambassador of the Emperor Charles V at the Court of Henry, in a letter [3] to his master (27 April, 1533) writes about this sermon with his usual accuracy and detail :—

" This feast of Easter, the prior of the Augustines [Geo. Browne] in his sermon recommended the people expressly to pray for Queen Anne ; at which they were astonished and scandalized, and almost every one took his departure with great murmuring and ill looks, without waiting for the rest of the sermon. The King was greatly displeased, and sent word to the Mayor that on dread of his displeasure he should take order that nothing of the kind happened

---

[1] *Harleian Miscellany*, v. 596.   [2] Harris, *Ware's Bishops*, 348.
[3] *L. and P. Hen. VIII*, 1533, no. 391.

again, and that no one should be so bold as to murmur at his marriage. The Mayor thereupon assembled the trades and their officers of the several halls [gilds], and commanded them, on pain of the King's indignation, not to murmur at his marriage, and to prevent their apprentices from so doing, and, what is worse and more difficult, their wives."

It is not to our purpose to dwell on the temper of the people in refusing to listen to Browne's approval of the King's marriage with Anne Boleyn. In this approval, Browne was justifying his own action, as, according to Chapuys, it was he who performed the ceremony on that occasion.[1] Here we see the hand of friendship held out by Cromwell to Browne in having him selected for such an important function and thus bringing him prominently before the eyes of the King. Cromwell sought promotion for his friend, and it was not long delayed.

OXFORD AND CAMBRIDGE CONFER DOCTORATE ON BROWNE.

Meanwhile, Browne was making use of his friendship with Cromwell to awaken the latter's interest in the University of Oxford. In a letter (March, 1534) which he sent by hand, from London, to Cromwell, he makes a poor show in trying to conceal his underhand dealings with the University. The letter [2] reads as follows :—

Our father and Mr. Provincial have written to me by this bearer to bring " this master and friend on to your speech and to instand your good mastership to be good unto the university," as your goodness is known to every man. The whole university, out of love for your mastership, have, without solicitation, given me " my incorporation of doctor *simpliciter* " without costs or charges. I beg you to thank the bearer for his [trouble] for your sake.

[1] *Letter*, 28 *Jan.*, 1535. *L. and P. Hen. VIII*, no. 121. The exact date of the marriage does not appear. Cranmer says " about St. Paul's Day " (25 Jan., 1533), but it was not until 29 May that Cranmer declared the marriage lawful. The coronation took place on 1 June, and on 7 Sept. the Princess Elizabeth was born. It would seem that Browne was called in to perform a secret marriage in January. Dr. Gairdner (*Lollardy and the Reformation*, i. 452) states, on the authority of Harpsfield, that it was Roland Lee (afterwards Bishop of Coventry and Lichfield) who performed the ceremony. Chapuys, who had inside information in Court affairs, is probably the more reliable authority.

[2] *L. and P. Hen. VIII*, vol. vii., no. 404.

It was a cunning piece of business on the part of Browne. He received the coveted Master of Theology [1] which would raise him in the eyes of his royal patron and of his friend ; he was attracting his friend's favour to Oxford University which evidently was in need of it at this time, and he was soliciting a favour for the bearer of the letter, and thus pleasing his own provincial. Cambridge University did not delay in following the good example of Oxford, and counted him among its theological doctors. [2]

Favours now began to be showered on Browne, and the King saw in him a useful instrument for the acknowledgment of his Royal Supremacy by the religious houses of the land.

BROWNE, VISITOR-GENERAL OF FRIARIES.

Within a month after Browne had received his degree from Oxford, he was the recipient of a royal grant (13 April, 1534) : [3] " Geo. Browne, prior of the Augustinian Hermits, London, appointed by the King provincial prior of the whole Order of Friars Hermits in England, and professor of Sacred Theology. Commission to himself and Hilsey to visit the houses of all friars of whatever Order . . . to make inquiry concerning their lives, morals, and fealty to the King, to instruct them how to conduct themselves with safety, and to reduce them to uniformity, calling in, if necessary, the aid of the secular arm."

Chapuys, who was always quick in obtaining information as to the King's movements, and quick in communicating them to his imperial master, wrote about a week afterwards (22 April) to Charles V :— [4]

The Archbishop of Canterbury [Cranmer] has begun to exercise his antipapality, making the bulls and despatch of three bishoprics, and he has by his own authority consecrated the three bishops. The King has also set in train the sovereignty to which he pretends over the English Church, and has appointed a Jacobin and an Augustinian [John Hilsey and Geo. Browne] provincials

---

[1] *Fasti Oxonienses*, i. 56 : " George Browne, a friar of the Order of St. Austen, and Doctor of Divinity of another University, was then incorporated Doctor of Divinity " (20 July, 1534).

[2] Chalmers' *Biog. Nat.*   [3] *Pat. 25 Hen. VIII*, p. 2, m. 6d.

[4] *L. and P. Hen. VIII*, 1534, no. 530.

and general visitors of all the religious, giving them among other
things the commission contained in the Bill hereto adjoined,
which will strike your Majesty as something very novel.

The Bill to which Chapuys refers is the Act of Supremacy,
the great Statute by which the new character of the Church
was defined. By the year 1534, Henry's quarrel with the
Pope had reached its height, and the severance of the Church
in England from its ancient dependence on Rome was complete. The Act ordered that the King " shall be taken,
accepted, and reputed the only supreme Head in earth of the
Church of England." Authority in all matters ecclesiastical,
as well as civil, was vested solely in the Crown. The " courts
spiritual " became as thoroughly the King's courts as the
temporal courts at Westminster. But the full meaning that
Cromwell attached to the Supremacy was seen on his eleva-
tion to the new post of Vicar-General, or Vice-gerent of the
King in all matters ecclesiastical. He was thus, a mere
layman, placed above the archbishops and bishops, even in
convocation and other strictly ecclesiastical assemblies.

There remained, therefore, no further obstacle to prevent
the King's dealing according to his royal pleasure with the
friars. He conceived the ingenious plan of appointing over
them a general superior upon whose faithful subservience to
himself he could depend. As a first step, Cromwell and his
master selected two worthy instruments, John Hilsey, a
Dominican friar, afterwards successor to the saintly John
Fisher in the See of Rochester, and George Browne. Cranmer
had previously begun that visitation of his province which
had for its object the obtaining of the signatures of the clergy
to the declaration that the Bishop of Rome had no greater
jurisdiction in England than any other foreign bishop. This
was generally obtained, and was also secured from the Uni-
versities of Oxford and Cambridge, and from the monasteries.
As it was judged necessary to obtain it also from the friars,
the above commission was issued to Browne and Hilsey
empowering them to visit the friars of all Orders and require
the signature of every inmate. The Franciscans offered a
stout resistance, and seven houses of the Observants (Reformed Franciscans) were cleared of their inhabitants, and
the more refractory members were sent to the Tower, some

of them hanged at Tyburn, while the less obstinate brethren were transferred to houses of the unreformed Order and were there loaded with chains.[1]

The members of the friaries, having been assembled in their chapter-houses, were examined separately concerning their faith and their obedience to the King and Anne Boleyn. Having made their grand tour, the visitors drew up the following report :—

Declaration of obedience to Henry VIII and queen Anne, and of the lawfulness of their marriage, with a repudiation of the bishop of Rome's authority, and acknowledgment of the King as Supreme Head of the Church, by the convents of the Franciscan, Dominican, Augustinian, Carmelite, and Crutched Friars of London under the signatures of the priors, namely, of Edmund Streatham, prior [of the Crutched Friars], Robert Strowddyll, S.T.P., prior of the Dominicans, George Burnham, prior of the Carmelites, Thomas Cudner, warden of the Friars Minors, and Geo. Browne, S.T.P., prior of the Augustinians. Dated in their chapter-houses, 17 April, 1534.[2] Acknowledged in chancery by the above heads of houses before Geo. Browne, prior provincial of the Augustinians, and John Hylsey, prior provincial of the Order of Friars Preachers, on the 17, 18, 20 April, *an. presen.*

Similar declarations were made, 6, 9, 16 May, by the convents of the Friars Preachers, Langley Regis, the Minors of Alisbury, the Preachers of Dunstable, the Minors of Bedford, the Carmelites of Hechynge, and the Minors of Ware, and afterwards in chancery before Browne and Hilsey. Other declarations were made by the prioress and convent of Dertford, Kent, diocese of Rochester.

The two visitors had made no delay in executing their commission. Within four days they had got the declaration of the London friaries in the chapter-houses, and within a week in chancery, and those of the southern parts of England within a month. Besides the above declaration, the religious were bound to swear solemnly that they would preach and persuade the people to accept the royal supremacy, and to confess that the Bishop of Rome had no more power than any other bishop, and to call him Pope no longer. Further, the sermons of each preacher severally were to be carefully

---

[1] See Fletcher, *op. cit.*, p. 77.   [2] *L. and P. Hen. VIII*, 1534, no. 665.

examined, and if not orthodox they were to be burned.[1] Every friar was to be strictly enjoined to commend the King as head of the Church, the Queen, the Archbishop of Canterbury, and the clergy to the prayers of the faithful. Lastly, each house was " to be obliged to show its gold, silver, and other moveable goods, and deliver an inventory of them," and to take a common oath, sealed with the convent seal, to observe the above orders.

Cromwell's was the master mind, of Machiavellian type, which first conceived the idea of attacking the papal power in its strongholds, the monasteries, and of procuring thereby the wealth to gratify the covetousness of the King.[2] Perhaps no actor on the stage of history has ever possessed greater powers, personal and political. He had been employed by Wolsey in the work of suppressing the monasteries, and acquired great experience of these houses. He escaped the fate of Wolsey by pointing out to Henry the way of getting rid entirely of allegiance to the Pope.

[1] Gasquet, *Hen. VIII and the English Monasteries.*

[2] Of the two men, Thomas Legh and Richard Layton, whom Cromwell sent into the north of England to visit the monasteries as distinct from the friaries, a writer in the *Athenæum* of 1886 says : " Seldom in the world's history has a tyrant found baser instruments for his basest designs than Henry found for carrying out the visitations of the English monasteries. That any monastery in England contained half a dozen such wretches as the more prominent of the visitors who came to despoil them is almost inconceivable. It is a sickening story. The reader is in danger of disbelieving everything that these men report in his indignation at the audacious and manifest lying which characterizes their reports," and Fletcher *(op. cit.,* p. 33) says that they " were adepts at bullying and cajoling—for they used both methods—the heads of the various institutions on which they descended." And Dr. Whitney (*The Reformation*) remarks : " It must be said that the evidence upon which the monasteries were condemned invites, and the agents who destroyed them compel, suspicions of the good faith of the Government." Again he says : " The Monastic Orders may have lost their former zeal, but they had not sunk to the low level of life that satirists and unfounded tradition ascribed to them." It may be observed that Dr. Whitney is the present Dixie Professor of Ecclesiastical History at Cambridge. And Dr. Gairdner, the editor of the *State Papers of Henry VIII,* with Dr. Brewer, after remarking (*Lollardy and the Reformation*) that the tradition against monasticism which has existed in England from the seventeenth to the nineteenth century arose from old nourished prejudices against men defenceless after they were dead, sums up the whole case in a sentence : " The defaming of the monasteries was simply a step towards their suppression and the confiscation of their endowments ; and apart from the gratification of avarice, their suppression was a necessary step in the policy which the King and Cromwell had been carefully engineering."

BROWNE, MASTER-GENERAL OF RELIGION.

Browne now assumed the position of Master-General of all the religious houses in England, and appointed friar Olyver as prior of the Black Friars at Cambridge. Cranmer in a letter to Cromwell (7 June) found fault with this appointment as Olyver had preached against the King's cause and defended the authority of the Bishop of Rome, and begged Cromwell to remove Olyver from this office and give it to Hilsey.[1] Whatever may have been the reason of Browne's appointment of Olyver, it is quite clear that Hilsey and Browne had not been agreeing of late, and that Hilsey resented this assumption of power by Browne. He complained of it in a letter [2] to Cromwell (16 Oct.), saying that Cromwell had appointed him (Hilsey) to the office of master-general, and that Browne had " broken certain assignations made by our general chapter, saying he is our master-general and we shall do nothing but under him."

Browne, however, was employed alone by Cromwell as bearer of letters [3] (15 June) to Bishop Roland Lee and Thos. Bedyll appointing them as commissioners to Richmond and Greenwich to receive submission to the King, as Head of the Church in England, from the convents of St. Francis there.

A few weeks afterwards Browne was again busy in visiting religious houses and taking their submission. Of this expedition he sends a report [4] to Cromwell, 6 July :—

Came on the 4 July to Beverley [S.E. Yorkshire] and visited the Grey and Black Friars, " where all did agree according to my commission." One Grey Friar, named Dr. Gwynborne, whome he has sent to Cromwell by the bearer, has written divers libels against the King, especially one " not only seditious, but much presueus [presumptuous ?] and of high stomach," which he has presented to the King : yet he would have sworn to me, but I did not take his oath. He pretended to have no knowledge ; but on my interrogating him, he confessed he knew that the Queen was crowned and had a princess. " Why then," said I, " did you write so shameful a book against this just matrimony and the book the which the Council set forth ? " He said he wrote according to his conscience, and confessed that his conscience confirmed it

---

[1] *L. and P. Hen. VIII*, 1534, vol. vii., no. 807.
[2] *Ib.*, no. 1265.   [3] *Ib.*, no. 841.   [4] *Ib.*, no. 953

all. [Brown] sends all his writings and copies. Thinks he has given copies about. He is a lunatic, or in a frenzy, as you will see if you common [commune] with him. [Browne] sends a register of all his goods and books. Thinks the writings are not his own composition, for he owns he is " poorly booked and poorly learned."

To-day, 6 July, I took my journey towards Newcastle ; received all the convent seals hitherto with loving thanks. I beg you to favor the bearer who is my kinsman born in the same town.

Rarely did Browne write a letter to Cromwell that he did not ask a favour for some relative or attendant of his own. However, he again returned to London and, within a few days, he and Hilsey were appointed by the King (16 July) as visitors to the friars of Southampton. For the next few months nothing is chronicled about his doings, but evidently he was busy and taking upon himself the sole work of visitation. It was on 16 October that Hilsey complained to Cromwell about Browne's attitude in this respect.

The Act of Supremacy had, indeed, added greatly to the royal power, and there was no pretence that it was framed with any scrupulous concern for civil liberty. By the beginning of 1535 any doubts that might have been entertained as to the full intentions of Henry were at an end. On 15 January, the new title of " Supreme Head " was incorporated in the King's style by decree of Council, though the rupture with Rome and the causes that led to it were unquestionably deeply distasteful to the English nation at large.[1]

Chapuys, in his regular correspondence with the Emperor Charles V, gives an account of this latest movement of the King, in a letter [2] of 28 January, 1535 :—

[1] " History shows that up to the very eve of the rejection of the Papal Supremacy, the attitude of Englishmen, in spite of difficulties and misunderstandings, had been persistently one of respect for the Pope as their Spiritual head. No doubt there were at times disagreements and quarrels, but these were rather in the temporal domain, without affecting the real attitude and uninterrupted spiritual dependence of England on the Holy See. . . . The claim of authority by the Popes to determine matters more or less of the temporal order tended to obscure the higher and supernatural powers which are the enduring heritage of St. Peter's successors in the See of Rome. To the ordinary man, the distinction between the necessary and the accidental prerogatives was not clear, and when one was called in question the other was imperilled. Moreover, English national feeling had grown by leaps and bounds in the early years of the 16th century " (Gasquet, *Eve of the Reformation*, pp. 73 ff.).

[2] *L. and P. Hen. VIII*, 1535, no. 121.

The King has added to his titles that of Sovereign Head of the Church of England on earth, and it is proposed to burn all the bulls and provisions hitherto granted by the Holy See. With this view, on Sunday last, an Augustinian friar [Dr. Geo. Brown] who has been appointed by the King general of all the Mendicent Orders in reward for having married the King and the Lady [Anne Boleyn], preached a very solemn sermon maintaining that the bishops and all others who did not burn all their bulls obtained from the Holy See, and get new ones from the King, deserved very severe punishment, and that without that they could not discharge any episcopal duty; that the sacred chrism of the bishops would be inefficacious, as made by men without authority, seeing that they obeyed the bishop or idol of Rome, who was a limb of the devil; and that to-morrow or after, it would be a question whether to rebaptise those baptised during that time. This language is so abominable that it is clear it must have been prompted by the King or by Cromwell, who makes the said monk his right-hand man in all things unlawful.

By the word " abominable " Chapuys evidently means heretical. He means that Browne knew enough theology not to be the author of such doctrines, and indeed not to believe in them himself. Browne could scarcely believe that the consecration of bishops without the King's sanction was invalid, and that ordinations of priests by such bishops were invalid. Nor indeed could he hold that baptisms performed by those priests would be invalid. Yet, in his sermon, he gives expression to these beliefs; but Chapuys shrewdly says that he believes he was prompted to them by either the King or Cromwell. By instilling these beliefs into the minds of the common people it was calculated that the Pope's authority would be undermined in no uncertain fashion, and thus the road would be cleared for the acceptance of the King as Supreme Head.

In other ways, too, continental Protestantism was obtaining a hold, and the Sacrament of the Altar [1] was becoming a subject of debate and doubt.

---

[1] " William Broman says that he has learned from the teaching of Dr. Barret, sometime a White Friar of Ipswich, about three or four years past [1531-2] that the Sacrament of the Altar is but a figure and remembrance of the Passion of Christ, and that the lifting up of the Host betokened only the sending down of the Son by the Father to suffer death for man; and the lifting up of the Chalice signified that the Father of Heaven sent down his Son to shed his

Browne and Hilsey seem to have been again employed by Cromwell to obtain recognition of the King's new title. In some notes of Cromwell (March, 1535), it is stated that the oath and form of profession of the bishops were to be delivered to the prior of Augustine Friars (Browne) and to the provincial of the Black Friars (Hilsey), so that they might have such oath and profession taken by all the Orders of Friars throughout the land.[1] Whether or when these visitors carried out such instructions does not appear. The visitations might have taken place between March and July. Meanwhile, Browne was with the Court at Richmond and employed as special preacher to the King. He was so busy that he was unable to go to see Cromwell over an important matter that had arisen in connection with the abbot of Meryvall and Mr. Turoylle (Tirylle). He wrote[2] to Cromwell (6 March) asking him to defer this matter until he is able to come in person and state his case. This will be, he says, immediately after he has preached before the King on the morrow. If he could, he would have come now and returned again to Court. But he tells Cromwell a few things about my lord of Meryvall. He says that when Cromwell's letters were delivered to that abbot, the latter declared that Cromwell was not his visitor, and that he would ask counsel of the fathers of his abbey. Browne concludes by saying that he has certain shameful accusations against the abbot.

CROMWELL AND CRANMER DISCUSS DOCTRINAL MATTERS.

Doctrinal matters were now being discussed by those at the head of affairs, and continental Protestants were being consulted by the English " reformers." As far back as July,

blood for man's salvation. That one Bale, a White Friar, sometime prior of Doncaster [afterwards Bishop of Ossory], taught him about four years ago that Christ would dwell in no church made of lime and stone by man's hands, but only in heaven above, and in man's heart in earth. That last Lent the parson of Hathfield taught the same doctrine, adding that no man ought to put trust in the Host when it was lifted up, but to remember and trust in the Passion of Christ. He had heard it reported by a dozen at least that the said parson preached that Our Lady was not Queen of Heaven, but the mother of Christ, and could do no more for us than another woman, likening her to a saffron bag. By his sermon he turned a hundred men's hearts to his opinion " (*L. and P. Hen. VIII*, 1535, vol. viii., no. 230).

[1] *Ib.*, no. 345.   [2] *Ib.*, no. 351.

1534, these intrigues were taking place. Chapuys in a letter [1] to Charles V (15 July, 1534) says that—

the ambassadors of Lubeck and Hamburg had a conversation with Cranmer and Cromwell, and [he] was told that the chief subject of their conversation was about certain articles of the Lutheran sect, both relating to the Pope and other things, on which those here wished to consult the doctor of Lubeck and to consider the best means of enforcing them among the people. This is very probable, because the above-named persons are the most perfect Lutherans in the world. I will inquire about it all I can.

In a second letter [2] Chapuys remarks that—

the doctor of Hamburg, whom those of Lubeck promised to bring here, has come, and it is said that the King has sent for Melanchton and another.

In another letter of September,[3] Chapuys states that—

the ambassadors of Lubeck and Hamburg have returned, leaving here three doctors to decide the rest of the articles, already mentioned, and to discuss the whole at the coming Parliament. They are at present occupied in writing on the question of the [Blessed] Sacrament. God grant that they may conclude about it and about confession otherwise than the world expects.

Again, in March, 1535, Chapuys writes :—[4]

matters of Church and of the Faith get worse every day. On Sunday last one preached before the King, and said openly that the King would do well to assemble the doctors of his realm, and determine whether in the consecrated host was the real (?) body of God (*le preneulx* [precious] *corps de Dieu*), and whether there was a purgatory ; and for his part he would not say till the said assembly.

It would seem that the preacher mentioned by Chapuys was none other than Browne who, as has been seen, was engaged in preaching before the King in that very month of March. If this be so, it will help to explain Browne's attitude towards the Mass during his occupation of the See of Dublin. He seems to have been permeated with continental Protestantism since his return to England. On the other

---

[1] *L. and P. Hen. VIII*, 15 July, 1534, no. 980.
[2] *Ib.*, 27 July.   [3] *Ib.*, September.   [4] *Ib.*, no. 355.

hand, it is scarcely necessary to remark that but a few years previously Henry had upheld the doctrine of Transubstantiation against Luther and received from the Pope the title "Defender of the Faith." And now he allows a preacher in his presence to cast a doubt upon the doctrine. But we shall see later how he put a stop to this Lutheran propaganda.

Meanwhile, Cranmer and Cromwell were attempting to carry out their scheme of greater "reform" than the King had a taste for. The following articles[1] drawn up for this purpose are found in the State Papers :—

How the false heresies which the bishop of Rome hath taught the people should be brought out of their conscience and hearts. 1. The archbishop of Canterbury should summon a council of bishops and doctors, and have them sign their decision on each of the articles contained in the "book of the charge." Which done, copies should be sent to each county with command to every sheriff, *custos rotulorum* and justice of the peace, to have them read at every session and great leet [court]. All parish churches should be visited, and the curates examined how they instruct the people. Let six or seven masters of the Chancery, "of the right sort, nothing favoring the Pope's laws, nor having living thereby," be appointed to judge questions of heresy. And let sermons in English be drawn up and appointed to be preached by the curates every Sunday.

Pamphlets against the doctrines of celibacy of the clergy, honoring of images and prayers for the dead to be printed before Parliament begins.

Bills to be drawn against the next Parliament :—
1. Allowing priests to marry and to work for their living.
2. Prohibiting on a penalty of £10 all offerings to images.

These were probably Cromwell's notes and showed his leaning towards Lutheranism. But he was never able to carry them into effect. Henry's "Six Articles" put a stop to these efforts.

Browne now began to occupy himself with other doctrinal matters besides the Supremacy of the Pope.

BROWNE'S SERMONS ON PURGATORY.

He was back in London in the month of July (1535) and was appointed by Cromwell to preach in the Cathedral. The

[1] *L. and P. Hen. VIII*, vol. vii., no. 1043.

Bishop of London, John Stokesley, hearing of this, sent the following letter [1] to Cromwell on 17 July :—

Because I had perfect knowledge four days ago that this provincial of the Friars [Geo. Browne] was appointed to preach and rail this Sunday, not only in reproach of me and my order, but also to maintain his indiscreet fashion of remembrance of the souls departed, I appointed Mr. Symons to preach, and sent for the Friar, requiring him to conform himself in praying for the souls departed as Mr. Latamer, Croome, and others did, or else to forbear this day. He made no answer. I beg, therefore, that Mr. Symons may preach, and when I am departed I shall suffer the Friar to rail at the Cross at his pleasure. He will set forth more fervently some pernicious doctrine unless he do all things very weakly ; for he has neither authority nor argument in these matters. If he preach to-morrow it will be with such contumely to me (such is his rashness) that I shall think all my services in this matter little regarded if in my presence he be maintained to excite sedition against me in my own church. Let him take his pleasure at home, and give public warning. If, after my departure, he contaminate my church, it shall less offend me.

My chaplain has just showed me that your pleasure was for an order " which, though I suspect that he shall utter this prior's ware," yet, for your sake, I am content to suffer him this Sunday ; but do not be displeased with me if his sermon be hereafter replied unto if he speak intolerably, as I hope, being by you beforehand, he will not.

It would appear from this that Browne had set out on a new crusade, namely, against the doctrine of Purgatory, in conformity with the articles of " reform " drawn up by Cromwell, and that he was far in advance of the other " reformers " who offered prayers for the dead in the old Catholic manner. It is clear that he had been preaching his own doctrine in other churches, probably, in Austin Friars, and that the Bishop, having heard about it, was much displeased. And it was too much for the latter when Browne was appointed to preach this doctrine in the Bishop's own cathedral. Stokesley made a dignified attempt to prevent this, but against such a man as Cromwell it was useless. Nevertheless, he warns Cromwell that he will not let the sermon go without replying

[1] *L. and P. Hen. VIII*, vol. vii., no. 1054.

to it. His poor opinion of Browne's theological learning is quite illuminating. He had evidently heard all the arguments put forward by the friar and thought them of no weight or authority. One thing apparent from all this is that Browne stood in high favour with the Vice-gerent Cromwell. That he was preaching to order is sufficiently clear, and Chapuys [1] easily guessed the source of his inspiration. Cromwell had been questioning the bishops one after another to see how much ecclesiastical authority they would concede to the head of the State, and at a special Council required their opinion whether the King could not by his own authority make and unmake bishops.[2] Of course if any of them had said No, the validity of his denial would immediately have been brought to the test ; so as to preserve their dignities they all replied in the affirmative. Cromwell himself confessed privately that that Council had been summoned only to entrap the bishops.[3] The Machiavellian policy of Cromwell is everywhere apparent.

Browne's sermons seem to have been the crown of all his efforts in pushing on the " reform " outlined by Cranmer and Cromwell. Browne was the energetic, unscrupulous instrument that Cromwell required for his schemes. The Archbishopric of Dublin was now vacant, and as, so far, the " reform " had had no promoter in Ireland, Browne was considered the one man who would be capable of pushing it on, and bringing that intractable land into line with England.

Browne Appointed Archbishop of Dublin.

Through the influence of Cromwell and Lord Rochford, Anne Boleyn's brother, Browne was chosen by the King to be Archbishop of Dublin. The See had been allowed by the King to remain vacant for nineteen months, during which time he took the profits of the temporalities. The Congé d'élire was granted at Eltham on 28 December, 1535, to the " Dean and chapter of the metropolitan church of Dublin," but was not issued from Westminster until 11 January of the following year. Though the election was nominally free,

[1] L. and P. Hen. VIII, 1535. Letter re Browne's Sermons.
[2] Ib., Intr., vol. ix., p. 25.   [3] Ib., no. 121.

the King's recommendation of Browne settled the matter, and the Chapters of St. Patrick's and Christ Church unanimously elected him. The royal sanction was granted on the 4 March, 1536, and on the 13th, the order was given for his consecration. On Sunday the 19th, Browne was consecrated in the chapel of Lambeth by Thomas Cranmer, Archbishop of Canterbury, Nicholas Shaxton, Bishop of Salisbury, and John Hilsey, Bishop of Rochester.[1] The same day he was invested by the same prelates with the pallium and in accordance with an Act then lately passed, and the certificate of his confirmation and consecration was issued. In all this, of course, there was no reference to Rome, as Henry had already constituted himself Head of the Church. But the conferring of the pallium, the symbol of the bond of union between an archbishop and the See of Peter, was certainly singular.

Browne, having taken the usual oath of fealty to the King, had the temporalities of his See restored to him on 23 March. A writ was sent to the Lord Chancellor of Ireland commanding him to issue a mandate accordingly to the several escheators of the counties of Dublin, Meath, and Louth where the temporalities lay. On the same day another writ was issued to the escheator of the county of Stafford to restore to him the temporalities of the archbishopric within the escheator's bailiwick, namely, the revenues of Penkridge Chapel of which the archbishops of Dublin were deans.[2]

PARLIAMENT AT DUBLIN ; ACTS FOR THE " KING'S ADVANTAGE AND THE COMMON WEAL."

Meanwhile, the Council of Ireland had thought it full time that this country should fall into line with England in the matter of " reform." On 16 June, 1535, Lord-Deputy Skeffington and Council wrote to the King informing him that they were sending over John Alen, Master of the Rolls, and Gerald Aylmer, Chief Baron of the Exchequer, with Acts for an Irish Parliament. These articles were declared to be " for the King's advantage and for the common weal of

---

[1] *L. and P. Hen. VIII*, vol. x. ; Rymer, *Fœdera*, xiv. 560 ; Harris, *Ware's Bishops*, 348.
[2] Rymer, xiv. 561 ; *Pat. 27 Hen. VIII*, m. 1.

the land and reformation."[1]   It was felt that Parliament alone could bring about their acceptance.

A few months afterwards (10 Oct.), Cromwell sent to Alen a commission to hold a Parliament and pass an Act acknowledging the King as head of the Church.[2]   A similar commission was sent to Lionel Gray from the King appointing him Lord-Deputy and commanding him to hold a Parliament. This commission was brought by Thomas Alen, brother of the Master of the Rolls.[3]   As the new Lord-Deputy was then engaged in suppressing the remains of the Geraldine revolt, nothing was done to open Parliament.   But the transactions of a recent Parliament at Westminster informed the " Irish subjects " what Acts would be most acceptable to the King. These were afterwards made the model of the ordinances of the Irish Parliament.

The commission received by John Alen for the holding of the Parliament is contained in the following receipt :—

This Bill indented, made the tenth day of October, in the 27th year [1535] of the reign of our Sovereign Lord King Henry VIIIth witnesseth that I, John Alen, Master of the Rolls in Ireland, have received of the right honourable Mr. Thomas Cromwell, Principal Secretary to our said Sovereign Lord, two patents, one of creation for Thomas Eustace, another like to Sir Richard Power, of Barons of Parliament in Ireland : a commission for holding of a Parliament within the same land, with certain schedules thereunto annexed, of causes and considerations of Acts to be passed in the said Parliament ; that is to say, an article for the attainder of the Earl of Kildare and others ; for the First Fruits ; for the granting of the subsidy ; to make the King Supreme Head of the Church

---

[1] *Cal. S.P.I., Hen. VIII*, p. 13.   The word " reformation " was used in the material sense.   With regard to the common weal of the land, Cox says : " He [Alen] was instructed to inform the king about the decay of the land, and that neither the English order, tongue, or habit, nor the king's laws are used above 20 miles in compass.   That this decay was occasioned, among other things, by the taking of coyn and livery without order ; that they want English inhabitants who formerly had arms and servants to defend the country ; but of late, the English proprietors had taken Irish tenants who can live without bread or good victuals, and expelled the English.   The country is all Irish, without order, security, or hospitality.   The making of a native chief governor [Earl of Kildare], and the frequent change of lord-deputy, are great faults. The greatest grievance is the alienation of crown lands, so that the king's revenue is not sufficient to defend the realm " (*Hib. Angl.*, i. 225).

[2] *Cal. S.P.I., Hen. VIII*, p. 15.   [3] *State Papers, Hen. VIII*, ii. 306.

there ; for the King's succession : the act for declaration of Treasons : another for taking away tributes, censes, dispensations, and all other jurisdictions from the Bishop of Rome ; for pursuing of appeals into England, and not to the Bishop of Rome ; a Resumption of certain possessions to the King : a Repeal of Poyning's Act,[1] etc.

It will be seen that these acts differ somewhat from those afterwards drawn up and reported to Cromwell by Brabazon.[2]

Parliament was opened at Dublin on Monday, 1 May, 1536, and on the following Sunday (7 May) Gray informed Cromwell by letter[3] " that the Parliament began here the last Monday, and such matters as yet hath been preferred for our Sovereign Lord the King goeth forward without any stop, and I doubt not but all the rest concerning His Grace shall have like expedition. Howbeit, according your mind to me, there be divers things deferred, waiting the coming of the Chief Justice and Master of the Rolls."

About a fortnight after its opening the Acts to be passed were finally drawn up and communicated by Brabazon to Cromwell (17 May, 1536) in the following letter :—[4]

Pleaseth it your honourable mastership to be advertised that these acts subsequent be passed the Common House : the act of attainder ; the act of the King's succession ; the act of the first fruits ; the act of the Supreme Head ; the act of slander ; the act of appeals ; an act of the lands of the Duke of Norfolk, my lord of Wiltshire, my lord of Shrewsbury, and other, with the possessions, as well of the spiritualities as the temporalities of such religious houses in England, as had any possessions, tithes, or other hereditaments here ; the repealing of Poyning's Act ; an act for the Earl of Ossory. The proctors of the spiritualities somewhat do stick, in divers of these acts ; and loth they are that the King's grace should be Supreme Head of the Church. Divers of these acts are passed the Higher House, and lack nothing but the Royal Assent, which hath been deferred, because of the coming of the Master of the Rolls and the Chief Justice ; but their abode [delay] is so long that my Lord [Gray] now intendeth that the Royal Assent shall pass. The Common House is marvellous good for the King's causes, and all the learned men within the same be very good ; so that I think all causes concerning the King's Grace

---

[1] *S.P. Hen. VIII*, ii. 320, note.   [2] See below.   [3] *Loc. cit.*
[4] *Ib.*, p. 315. *Athen. Oxon.*, ii. 759.

will take good effect. In brief time your honourable mastership shall be certified of all such causes as here do pass.

And Gray in a letter [1] to Cromwell (21 May, 1536) states that—

The proceedings of the Parliament goeth forward in such wise as our said Sovereign Lord's pleasure is, so that divers acts be passed to the Royal Assent, and the same were stayed, waiting the coming of the Chief Justice, and Master of the Rolls; and by reason of their long tarrying it is thought good by me and the Council here that they shall pass.

Aylmer and Alen arrived in Dublin just a few days before Parliament was adjourned,[2] with the King's letters empowering Gray to give the royal assent to those Acts already passed. Parliament adjourned on the last day of May; "want of money prevents them [the Council] from repelling John of Desmond and O'Brien, and obliges them to adjourn the Parliament to Kilkenny." [3]

The Lord-Deputy and Council of Ireland in a letter [4] to Cromwell (1 June, 1536) state that they have adjourned the Parliament to Kilkenny against the 25 July, and thence to pass with the Army and all the strength of these quarters to the city of Limerick to proceed against Desmond, O'Brien, and others. They then mention that the following Acts, amongst others, had been passed in the Parliament : Act of Succession ; Act of Declaration of Treasons ; Act of Attainder of Earl of Kildare and others ; Act of Supreme Head ; Repeal of Poyning's Act ; Act of the First Fruits ; Act of Appeals ; Act of Subsidy ; Act for the resumption of Leislepe.

(Signed) Leonard Gray ; John Barnewall (Chancellor) ; John Rawson, prior of Kilmainham ; William Brabazon ; Gerald Aylmer, Justice ; John Alen, Master of the Rolls ; Thomas Lutterell, Justice ; Patrick Fynglas, Baron ; Thomas Houth, Justice.

---

[1] S.P. Hen. VIII, ii. 318.

[2] Alen in a letter to Cromwell (20 May) tells him that he has arrived at Chester. He evidently arrived in Dublin during the following week, as on 29 May Gray, in a letter to the King, acknowledges receipt of the royal letters through the Chief Justice and the Master of the Rolls (Cal. S.P.I., Hen. VIII, p. 18).

[3] Ib., p. 19.   [4] S.P. Hen. VIII, ii. 319-20.

In these accounts it is useful to observe that the Parliament, in its first session, passed the Act of the King's Supremacy, but, it must be remembered, not without great opposition on the part of the spiritual lords and their proctors. Their opposition was not confined to this Act but extended to "divers of these Acts." Now, the only other Acts that they presumably objected to were the "Act of Appeals" to the Pope, and the "Act of the First Fruits." In the list of Acts drawn up as passed both Houses, these are included. It is not so clear that the Act of First Fruits was passed at this session. The *Annats*, as they were called, were usually paid to the Pope, and were the revenues for the first year coming to prelates, prebendaries, etc. Though appeals to the Pope had been abolished, it is not so clear that the Spiritual Lords deprived the Pope of these *Annats* which were an acknowledgment of his spiritual jurisdiction. Whatever they may have thought of the King as the Head of the Church in Ireland, for the control of ecclesiastical affairs, it is unfair to infer at this stage that they were cutting themselves off altogether from Rome. As to the First Fruits, the King in his instructions to the Commissioners (31 July, 1537) states that he wishes, among other Acts, "an Act for the payment of First Fruits" to be passed. And Cromwell wrote, on the same day, to the Sheriff of Wexford informing him that such an Act should be passed.[1] Thus, more than a year after the Parliament of May, 1536, the Act of First Fruits had evidently not been passed.[2]

ACTS OF SUCCESSION AND ABSENTEES.

Having drawn up an Act of Attainder [3] against the late Earl of Kildare, and the associates of his rebellious son, Parliament proceeded to adjust the right of succession to the Crown of England, and lordship of Ireland. They pronounced the

[1] *S.P. Hen. VIII*, ii. 452.

[2] Loftus MSS. (Marsh's Library) *ad an.* 1534, state : "Many first fruits were granted to the King by the clergy of Ireland."

[3] *Ir. Stat. 28 Hen. VIII*, c. 1. In this Act it is stated that "Thomas FitzGerald did send his letters addressed as well to the bishop of Rome, as the emperor, by one Cale mac Grauyll, otherwise called Charles Raynolde, archdeacon of Kelles, for to have their aid against our said sovereign lord and his heirs for the winning of the said land of Ireland out of their possession and he to hold the same of them for ever."

marriage of the King with Catherine of Arragon to be null
and void, and the sentence of separation by the Archbishop
of Canterbury to be good and effectual. They declared the
inheritance of the Crown to be in the King and his heirs by
Queen Anne ; pronounced it high treason to oppose this
succession, misprision of treason to slander it ; and drew up
an oath of allegiance to be taken by the subjects of Ireland
for the sure establishment of it.[1]

A few days after Parliament had been adjourned to
Kilkenny, Cromwell, in a letter (3 June, 1536) to Lord-Deputy
and Council, acknowledges receipt of Brabazon's letter which
set forth the Acts passed in Parliament, and adds that " in
case the Act for the Succession be not passed thoroughly,
ye shall stay the same till further knowledge of his Grace's
pleasure, which shall be shortly signified unto you in that
behalf," etc.

Brabazon had written on 17 May to Cromwell telling him
of the passing of this Act. This was only two days before
Anne Boleyn's execution. Before the letter reached London
Jane Seymour had already been Queen a full fortnight, and
Cromwell's concern was, if possible, to stop the passing of
an Act which would have to be repeated so soon. It was
too late to do this, but the Irish Parliament made no difficulty
about enacting the same stringent rule of succession for the
third as they had done for the second wife. They thus
achieved the unique distinction of passing two contradictory
Acts of Settlement within eighteen months. This remarkable
performance does not adorn the Statute Book, because that
compilation was made when Elizabeth, Anne's daughter,
was firmly seated on the throne.[2]

A very easy and effective means of providing for the
" King's advantage " was adopted in the Act of Absentees [3]
which vested in the King the honours and estates of the following who held lands in Ireland : the abbot of Furness, the abbot
of St. Augustine's of Bristol, the prior of Christ Church,
Canterbury ; the prior of Lanthony, the prior of Cartinel, the

---

[1] *Loc. cit.*, c. 2.
[2] See Bagwell, *Ireland under the Tudors,* i. 196. The contemporary
Schedue of the Acts is in *S.P.* ii. 526.
[3] *Ir. Stat.*, c. 3.

abbot of Kentesham, the abbot of Osney, the abbot of Bath, and the master of St. Thomas of Dacres, besides the Duke of Norfolk and other absentee landlords.

The weakening of the English power in Ireland by the non-residence of great proprietors had long been recognised. Edward III, on the occasion of his son Lionel's mission, announced by proclamation that the lands of absentees would be granted to Englishmen willing and able to defend them against the Irish. The momentous Act now passed declared that many great proprietors had notoriously failed to defend their lands, whereby the King was forced to incur great expense in bringing an army to Ireland. All their property was resumed to the Crown, saving the rights of residents in Ireland, who held under the dispossessed lords. The Crown thus became one of the greatest of Irish landlords, and the foundations of a reconquest were laid.

REPEAL OF POYNING'S ACT.

By a Statute (10 Henry VII, chap. 4) commonly called Poyning's Act, it had been ordained " that no Parliament should thenceforth be holden in Ireland, till the King's lieutenant and council should first have certified to the King, under the great seal of the land, the causes and considerations, and all such Acts as them seemed should pass in the Parliament; and should have received the King's affirmation of their goodness and expediency, and his licence to summon the Parliament under the great seal of England." But soon after the opening of the present Parliament, Poyning's Act was declared to be repealed by the assent of the King ; and it was

enacted that this Parliament, and all its acts and ordinances should be valid, provided they should be thought expedient for the King's honour, the increase of his revenue, and the common weal of Ireland.[1]

In chapter 20 of the Irish Statutes of 28 Henry VIII, attention was paid to the doubt occasioned by the copulative *and* in the last clause of the provision (chap. 4). The provision in that Statute is, therefore, to be taken, that every

[1] *Ir. Stat.* 28 *Hen. VIII*, c. 4.

Act of this Parliament concerning either the King's honour and profit, or increase of his revenues, or otherwise concerning the commonwealth, shall be good in law, according to the tenor of that Statute.   It is a felony to attempt to avoid this Parliament, or such provisions thereof as aforesaid, after notice of this Act given by the judge where a suit for that purpose commenced, and such suit, etc., void.

The repeal of Poyning's law was passed, therefore, to validate the proceedings of this Parliament, though it had been held contrary to that law.   But the spirit, if not the letter of that famous measure, had been observed by preparing the Bills in England.   Indeed, the Parliament was absolutely subservient.   " The Common House," wrote Brabazon, " is marvellous good for the King's causes, and all the learned men within the same be very good ; so that I think all causes concerning the King's grace will take good effect." [1]

ACT AUTHORISING THE KING TO BE SUPREME HEAD OF THE CHURCH IN IRELAND.

An Act [2] was next passed authorising the King, his heirs and successors to be Supreme Head of the Church in Ireland :—

Like as the King's Majesty justly and rightfully is and ought to be supreme head of the Church of England, and so is recognised by the clergy, and authorised by an act of Parliament made and established in the said realm : so in like manner of wise, forasmuch as this land of Ireland is depending and belonging justly and rightfully to the imperial crown of England, for increase of virtue in Christ's religion within the said land of Ireland, and to repress and extirp all errors, heresies, and other enormities and abuses, heretofore used in the same ; be it enacted by authority of this present Parliament, That the King our sovereign lord, his heirs and successors, Kings of the said realm of England, and lords of this said land of Ireland, shall be accepted, taken, and reputed the only supreme head in earth of the whole church of Ireland, called (*Hibernica Ecclesia*) and shall have and enjoy, annexed and united to the imperial crown of England, as well the title and stile thereof, as all honours, dignities, preeminences, jurisdictions, privileges, authorities, immunities, profits, and commodities to

[1] Brabazon to Cromwell, 17 May, 1536.   [2] *Ir. Stat. Hen. VIII*, c. 5.

the said dignity of supreme head of the same church belonging and appertaining, and that our said sovereign lord, his heirs and successors, Kings of the said realm of England, and lords of this land of Ireland, shall have full power and authority from time to time to visit, repress, redress, reform, order, correct, restrain and amend all such errors, heresies, abuses, offences, contempts and enormities, whatsoever they be, which by any manner, spiritual authority, or jurisdiction, ought or may lawfully be reformed, restrained, [etc.] or amended, most to the pleasure of Almighty God, the increase of virtue in Christ's religion, and for the conservation of peace, unity, and tranquillity of this land of Ireland ; any usage, custom, foreign laws, foreign authority, prescription, or any other thing or things to the contrary notwithstanding.

Provided alway, and be it enacted by the authority of this present Parliament, That if it fortune our sovereign lord the King, his heirs or successors, to authorise and depute any person or persons to visit, repress etc. by force of the present and foresaid act, that then any such person or persons shall go with such company, as shall be convenient and necessary for the same ; and that according the ability, substance, and power of the person, house, or monastery, which they shall so fortune to visit, repress etc. ; and that no such person or persons so appointed or authorised to visit, repress etc., shall take or cause to be taken any process money, or other exactions of any such person, house, or monastery, which they shall so fortune to visit, repress etc., but only convenient meat, drink, and lodging for themselves, their company, servants, and horses ; and if any such person or persons, so appointed and authorised as aforesaid, do take or cause to be taken, any process money or any other exactions (other than is aforesaid) that every of them so offending shall forfeit four times the value of that that he receiveth or cause to be received, the one half thereof to our sovereign lord the King, his heirs and successors, and the other half to any person or persons that will sue for the same by action of debt, information, or otherwise, wherein no wager of law, essoine, nor protection shall lie.

An Act of Appeals.

An Act of Appeals [1] was introduced for the purpose of taking away all appeals to Rome in spiritual causes, and referring all such appeals to the Crown. It enacted :—

[1] *Ir. Stat. Hen. VIII*, c. 6.

Where divers good and wholesome laws and statutes be made
and established within the realm of England for the annulling and
utter taking away of appeals in cases spiritual from the bishop
of Rome and See Apostolic, and such other as claim by authority
of the same, not only for great speed of justice to the King's subjects of the said realm, but also in taking away the long delays,
costs, charges, and expenses that the said subjects sustained by
reason of such appeals ; [1] and forasmuch as this land of Ireland
is the King's proper dominion of England, and united, knit, and
belonging to the imperial crown of the same realm, which crown
of itself, and by itself, is fully, wholly, entirely, and rightfully
endowed, and garnished with all power, authority and pre-
eminence, sufficient to yield and render to all and singular
subjects of the same full and plenary remedies in all causes of
strife, debate, contention, or division, without any suit, provocation, appeal or any other process to be had, made, or sued to any
foreign prince or potentate spiritual or temporal : be it therefore,
and for the common weal of the subjects of this land, ordained,
and enacted by authority of this present Parliament, That no
person or persons, subjects or residents of this land, shall from
the first day of this present Parliament pursue, commence, use or
execute any manner of provocations, appeals, or other process,
to or from the bishop of Rome, or from the See of Rome, or
to or from any other that claim authority by reason of the
same, for any manner of case, grief, or cause, of what nature
soever it be, upon the pain that the offenders, their aiders, coun-
sellors, and abettors, contrary to this act, shall incur and run
into such pains, forfeitures, and penalties, as be specified and contained in the act of provision and premunire, made in the realm
of England in the 16th year of King Richard II,[2] sometime King

---

[1] We have already seen Alen's observation as to Wolsey's charges for dispensations compared to the expenses in receiving them from Rome (see *Introd.*).

[2] *An Act against Provisors to Rome* : " Praying the commons assembled
in this present Parliament, that where before this time there hath been, and yet
be within the said land of Ireland, many debates and strifes betwixt the prelates
and other of the church of Ireland, by reason of divers provisors suing by false
and untrue suggestions made unto the court of Rome, for to deprive and put
out of possession the said prelates and other beneficers from their livelihood
and benefices, and by colour and cause whereof many of the King's true subjects,
prelates and beneficers in that land, wrongfully by strength and might be put
out of their livelihood, and such persons provisors be put in their places, contrary
to the statutes of provision in that behalf ordained, and contrary to reason,
right, and good conscience ; Wherefore be it ordained, enacted, and established
by the authority of this present Parliament, That all manner of statutes, as
well made within the realm of England, as within the said land of Ireland,
against provisors, by the authority of this present Parliament, be authorised,

of England and lord of Ireland, against such as procure to the court of Rome or elsewhere to the derogation or contrary to the prerogative or jurisdiction of the said crown of England. And that no manner of person, subject or resident within this said land, shall attempt, procure, or obtain any manner of process, of what kind or nature soever it be, to or from the same bishop of Rome, or court of Rome, or See Apostolic, or from any other having authority by the same, nor in any wise obey or execute within this land such manner of process, upon like pains or forfeits as been above rehearsed.

It was further enacted that all such appeals in future shall be made

To the King of England and lord of Ireland, his heirs and successors, or to his or their lieutenant, deputy, justice, or other governor, whatsoever he be, of this land of Ireland for the time being, to his or their court of chancery within the said realm of England or land of Ireland . . . [who] shall grant a commission or delegacy to some discreet and well learned persons of this land of Ireland, or else in the realm of England, for final determination of all causes and griefs contained in the said provocations and appeals etc. And upon every such provocation, appeal [to aforesaid], the chancellor of this said land of Ireland, or keeper of the great seal of the same for the time being, by the assent of the chief justices of the king's bench and common place, the master of the rolls, and the undertreasurer of the said land for the time being, or to any two of them, so as the undertreasurer be one, shall grant a commission or delegacy to some discreet and well learned persons within this land of Ireland, for final determination of all causes and griefs contained in the said provocation etc.

In reference to these Acts, Robert Cowley, in a letter[1] to Cromwell (August, 1536), says :—

approved, and confirmed, and be deemed good and effectual in the law ; and also by authority aforesaid, That all and every of the statutes, made against provisors, be from henceforth duly and straightly executed in all points within the said land, according to the effect of the same. And the King's justices, and commissioners of the said land diligently enquire at their sessions, and all other times requisite and behoveful, of all and every manner of person or persons that hereafter offend the said statutes, or any of them, and every of the said persons so founden defective or trespassing in any of the said statutes, from henceforth be duly corrected and punished, in example of all other in time to come, according to the tenure and purport of the said statute " (*Rot. Parl.*, c. 10, *Ir. Stat.*, i. 45, 1495).

[1] *S.P. Hen. VIII, Ir.*, i. 366.

that your good Lordship would vouchsafe either to substitute under your Lordship some able person in Ireland to exercise your Lordship's high authority and faculties, or some part thereof, in Ireland ; or else to assign a certain person or persons in this realm to whom the suitors of Ireland might resort for expedition of their impetrations, whereof might grow a profit and a means to stop all marchers [borderers] and Irishmen from recourse to the Bishop of Rome. Item, that the King's deputy and council may have injunctions principally to prosecute all provisors going to Rome and papists with extreme punishment with all their authors and factors.

So as, in conclusion, they condescended that when the bills were passed the Common House the Speaker should deliver them to the Convocation House; but whether they agreed or not agreed they would nevertheless proceed to . . . whereunto we condescended the rather that . . . for the assurance to the King of the lands and p[ossessions that] lately appertained to the eight abbeys expressed in [the commission] [1] under the Great Seal of England [2] which by v[irtue thereof] according the King's pleasure we have lately supp[ressed].

The bill of the 20th part of the spirituality (whereunto at th[eir] session they assented) and divers others, being passed the Common House, and presented by the Speaker according the said determination, in the end the Spiritual Lords in the High House, conspiring together, denied to assent to any of the same, making r[esolute] answer, first to the Chancellor and after to us in . . . Parliament that they would not agree to the passing of [the said] Act.

There is no mention in the letter of the Council to Cromwell (1 June, 1536) that any Act for suppression of religious houses had been passed. This Act, as well as that of the 20th part of spiritualities, and the First Fruits, was evidently held up by the spiritual lords and proctors until a later session when the proctors of the bishops had been deprived of their vote. The Act for the 20th was not passed until about Easter, 1537. Likewise the Act of Faculties was not passed until the Act against the proctors had passed. It would seem that the commission, mentioned by Cowley, and brought by

[1] This portion of the letter is much mutilated.

[2] No minute or copy of this commission for the suppression of the eight religious houses having been found, search has been made for it on the Patent Rolls of 27, 28, and 29 Hen. VIII, but without success.

Alen and Aylmer, for the suppression of eight houses, was
not presented to Parliament, for fear of arousing too much
opposition. It was thought more discreet quietly to suppress
them in virtue of that commission and of the King's jurisdiction under the Supremacy Act. This was carried out,
according to Cowley. It was an experiment with a view to
further suppressions.

Browne about to Set Out for Dublin.

Whilst Parliament was being held at Dublin, Browne was
still in London getting his horses and retinue ready for his
journey to his See. In that month (May, 1536) he wrote a
letter to Cromwell which contains many points of great
importance. This letter [1] reads as follows :—

*To the right honourable Mr. Thomas Crumwell, High Secretary unto
the King's Highness.*

Right honourable sir, I desire you of your goodness as I have
been always singularly bound unto you, so now at this chiefest
point of all to stand by me and aid me in these extremes [extremi-
ties]. I have of long season (as your Mastership) knoweth full
well made daily suit unto you as concerning my departure unto
the promotion that it hath pleased the King's Highness of his
most abundant grace to grant and give unto me (at your Mastership's instant labour) in the parts of Ireland the which I cannot
attain without your Mastership. Be good unto me now as I have
always found your immortal benefits in times past, partly for the
consuete [usual] charges that I was at, even of duty paid by
custom of all that entereth unto any such room [i.e. the arch-
bishopric]. And since that of no small expenses diversely laid out,
both for necessaries concerning mine own person, and also my
servants' weekly board wages, besides the both costly price and
also the chargeable finding of so many horses as I intend (God
willing) and as very congruence [congruity] shall require to have
with me. I have besides this to commune with your Mastership
as concerning a certain matter betwixt my Lord of Rochford and
me. Sir, I hear how that Mr. Agar and other of that party be
despatched with favour ; wherefore I beseech your Mastership
for God's love to tender the cause [acquaint him] how and in

---

[1] *S.P. Hen. VIII*, vol. iii., no. 31, P.R.O., London. We have modernised
the spelling in this as in other letters.

what case I stand in.   It had been better for me never to have
been named [promoted] than thus utterly to be shamed.   I and
all mine be at your Mastership's commandment and pleasure.

Your poor orator and bedman,[1]

GEORGE BROWNE.

It seems strange that Browne signs himself simply " George
Browne " and not " George, Dublin " as he was entitled to
do, being already consecrated for that See.   The letter ex-
plains this point.   It was a friendly letter, a begging letter,
if we like to call it.   Browne had for a considerable time been
calling daily on Cromwell to consult him about his expenses
for his journey and how he was to meet them.   Evidently,
Cromwell was too busy or did not wish to be troubled about
such trifles.   Almost in despair, Browne, still in London, sent
this letter, probably, by hand, by one of his servants, and he
did not wish to assume any dignity in such a plight and especially towards his benefactor.

As to the date of the letter, it must be said that it is not
given in the original.   That is also explained by what we
have already said as to the sending of the letter by one of
Browne's servants.   In the State Papers it is given as belonging to May, 1536.   That seems reasonable, first because of
the position it occupies in the collection, and secondly because
it must come about midway between March (month of his
consecration) and July (month of his arrival in Dublin).
Moreover, it is confirmed by Browne's own words : " I have
of long season daily made suit unto you," probably, for a
month or more.

We have no reason to believe that Browne had amassed
any considerable wealth during his tenure of office in England as visitor-general.   And, no doubt, to gather together a
retinue of servants and horses, paying not only for the horses
and their equipment but for the buying of them, was a costly
business for him.   The wages of these men, their board and
lodging, the upkeep of the horses during the journey from
London to Holyhead, all these must have amounted to a large

---

[1] *Orator*, i.e. *petitioner* (Latin, *Oro*, I pray).   *Bêdman*, i.e. supplicant, one
who prays (Anglo-Saxon, *biddan*, to pray.   Ex. gr. to bid one's beads.)   A
curious mixture of Latin and Anglo-Saxon !

sum. Browne pleads his inability to pay. Besides he has to pay the usual fine to the King on entering into the Archbishopric, and, probably, a bonus to Cromwell also. Cromwell had undoubtedly been a constant friend of Browne, and presumably on this occasion he befriended the new Archbishop whom he had had appointed to the office.

The matter " betwixt my Lord of Rochford and me " is of special interest. Rochford was brother to Anne Boleyn whom Browne had worked hard to have recognised as lawful wife of Henry. Browne had made a compact with Rochford for the sum of £250 on condition that the latter used his influence with Henry through Anne to obtain Browne's promotion to the Archbishopric. What exactly Browne wished to mention to Cromwell about this deed does not appear, but it was probably in reference to Rochford's fall from power along with his sister. Evidently Browne expected to escape payment of the debt under the circumstances. We shall see later how this matter worked out.

But more interesting from the general historical standpoint is the complaint made by Browne in the last portion of his letter. The complaint was to the effect that Agard and another, Cromwell's servants, were being sent over to Ireland. No one knew better than Browne the Cromwellian system, and he thus saw these men as spies, which they undoubtedly were.[1] But, if they were to spy on his actions from the very moment when he was taking on his shoulders the burden of the Archbishopric of Dublin, then indeed, he declares, it were better for him never to have been appointed to such a position than thus to be made little of. But this was not all. Body, another of Cromwell's servants and spies, was even sent by his master to accompany Browne to Dublin. In a letter (1 July) to Cromwell,[2] Body tells how he hired a good ship at Westchester which was to be ready at Holyhead for the first

---

[1] " Thomas Cromwell," says Fletcher (*op. cit.*, p. 26), " in addition to being the most unscrupulous statesman that England has ever known, was also a perfect master of the spy system. No man was safe under the Cromwell régime. ' Early in 1532,' says Mr. Merriman, ' Cromwell began to create a system of espionage, the most effective that England had ever seen, that in a short time was to render unsafe the most guarded expression of dissent in politics or religion. The success which this organized method of reporting treason later obtained, is one of the most striking proofs of the relentless energy of its originator.' "

[2] *Cal. S.P. Ir.*, p. 21.

wind. And Browne, in a letter to the same (19 July) [1] tells
how he arrived in Dublin with Mr. Body on Saturday, 15 July.
There was other work for Body to do besides spying. He
received instructions from Cromwell to induce the Lord-Deputy
and Council to use every effort to increase the King's revenues
in Ireland. We shall see the means adopted by Gray in
Parliament to satisfy the wants of the penniless King.

Meanwhile Cromwell had not forgotten the begging appeal of Browne, and conferred a favour on him by having
restored to him the temporalities of the diocese from Michaelmas, 1535.   In a letter [2] to the Lord-Deputy and Council
of Ireland (3 June, 1536), Cromwell, having thanked them
for passing the Acts in Parliament, proceeds :—

Ye shall also understand that, for as much as the King's Majesty
hath given unto the Archbishop of Dublin the whole revenue due
of his Archbishopric since Michaelmas last passed, his pleasure is
that you, Master Brabazon, shall either deliver the same to the
said Body or else, in case it be employed in the King's affairs
there,[3] signify the certain sum thereof, to the intent it may be
deducted of such [sum as] shall shortly be sent thither. For ye
shall understand that his charges here [hath been] great, by reason
whereof he is much [endebted], and must discharge the same of
the [revenue] said bishopric unto him. For whom, in the mean-
time [I] have undertaken with all his creditors, and therefore
desire and pray you to take such order, as he may, either from
thence, or [otherwise] by your limitation, receive his duty accordingly.

From this it would seem that Cromwell had gone security
for Browne for all the debts he had incurred in fitting out his
retinue for their journey to Dublin, and that the Archbishop
was to pay these debts through Brabazon out of his temporalities.

Meanwhile Browne endeavoured to keep in the good

---

[1] *Loc. cit.*   [2] *S.P. Hen. VIII*, i. 330.
[3] Brabazon was the King's undertreasurer. In his account for the archbishopric from Alen's death until Michaelmas, 1535 (about one year), he gives
the receipts as £623 5s. 8d. Browne was thus granted the temporalities of
nine months (i.e. from Michaelmas, 1535, to June, 1536), or roughly about
three-fourths of this sum. As to the money having been employed in the King's
affairs, it is interesting to mention that Body stated that the Geraldine rebellion
cost the King above £40,000 sterling.

graces of Body and Agard, shamed though he was at Cromwell's want of trust in him. Indeed, as this history proceeds
it will be seen that neither his so-called friends of the " reform " nor his enemies had the least respect for him. Within
four days of his arrival in Dublin, Browne collated Body to
the richest benefice in his diocese, that of Swords. Lord-
Deputy Gray was furious over this promotion of a layman, and declared in a letter to Cromwell (24 Nov., 1536) [1]
that Browne had no right to do so and that he did it simply
to win over Body. Gray likewise tells how he brought
Body with him to the journey of Munster and the assault
of O'Brien's Bridge and entertained him " as if he had been
a great man." Body, with the insolence of a great man's
favourite, had throughout this expedition assumed the character
of a Royal Commissioner, to which he had not the shadow
of title. He blamed Gray for his methods of attack and afterwards sought to undermine his influence. Such was the agent
and spy sent over by Cromwell to report on Irish affairs, a
low drunkard, " full unmeet both in experience and temper-
ance, being once a day, commonly, in that case that I was
sorry to see it," namely, drunk. No wonder Gray held himself aloof, as much as possible, from the " religious reform "
which men like Browne, Alen, and Brabazon, aided by Cromwell's spies, Body and Agard, were endeavouring to push
forward. We shall see the development of these characters
as we proceed.

Though Browne arrived in Dublin in July, it was not until
December that he thought well to preach in his cathedral.
There is nothing to indicate the reason of his reluctance or
remissness. It may be that he did not find the people or his
clergy anxious to hear the doctrine of the King's Supremacy
preached. Parliament had removed from Dublin to the South
and, in the absence of the Council, and the consequent re-
vulsion of feeling against many of the Acts introduced, he
may have considered it rather venturesome to take any
determined step. But Parliament had returned to Dublin
on 15 September, and progress was being made in making
the Acts more acceptable. All this evidently had its effect

[1] *L. and P. Hen. VIII*, xi., no. 1157.

on Browne, and he preached his first sermon early in December. Martin Pelles tells us about it in a letter [1] to Cromwell (4 Dec., 1536): "The Archbishop of Dublin preached his first sermon in this land the Sunday after Saint Andrew (30 Nov.) in the Cree [Christ] Church, Dublin, and set forth the word of God so sincerely, that those men that be learned and unlearned both give him high praise. Those who favour the word of God are very glad of him."

Those who favoured "the word of God," in the opinion of Pelles, were, of course, the opponents of Rome.

COUNCIL OF IRELAND—JEALOUSY AND DISTRUST.

Besides obstinacy on the part of the spiritual lords and members of the Common House, there was another cause that prevented the carrying out of the King's wishes to their full extent. The Council of Ireland was composed of men who distrusted one another and who constantly complained to Cromwell about one another's line of action.

Immediately after the adjournment of Parliament, in a letter (1 June, 1536) [2] to Cromwell, they state :—

For although it hath been reported and bruited that division is among us of the Council here, we assure your Mastership there is no such matter, nor yet, by the grace of God, shall none be ; but that we are, and shall be, in one conformity about every of the King's affairs, as doth become us.

Signed, Barnewall, Rawson, Brabazon, Aylmer, Alen,
Lutterel, Fynglas, Howth. [3]

But this hope of the Lord-Deputy was not to be fulfilled. What with Agar and Body assuming place of authority as royal commissioners, and the Lord-Deputy, with Aylmer and Alen, also claiming superiority, the King's business was being obstructed in no uncertain fashion. A brief survey of the situation will be useful.

After the surrender of Lord Thomas Fitzgerald, Gray succeeded, to some extent, in winning over the other lords and chieftains to the King's peace. Con O'Neill agreed to

---

[1] *Carew Cal.*, p. 111.   [2] *S.P. Hen. VIII*, ii. 322.

[3] It is to be noted that Browne's name does not appear among the signatories, for the simple reason that he had not at this time arrived in Dublin.

serve the King against all rebels and enemies, and, according
to a letter from Gray to Cromwell, peace was concluded also
with O'Brien, O'Connor, O'More, McGillpatrick, and the
Geraldines. Gray recommended the granting of the forfeited
lands to those who held the King's peace, and the reduction
of the army. At the same time he recommended the conquest of McMurrough[1] O'Murroughoe, O'Byrne, O'Toole, and
their kinsmen inhabiting between Dublin and Wexford.[1]
The reduction of the army did not find favour with Brabazon,
the King's Treasurer in Ireland. Though the pay of the
soldiers was a year in arrears, Brabazon would prefer to see
a larger army and allow the soldiers to take loot and pay
themselves, as they requested. Gray, endeavouring to bring
about peace in the country, was friendly towards Ireland,
but Brabazon aimed at the conquest of the country by
spoliation.

Gray, in a letter to Cromwell (23 Nov., 1536), points out
jealousy in the Council, and mentions Body and Brabazon
as the chief causes. Yet, the next day, the Council, including
Gray, wrote to the King declaring there was no dissension in
the Council. Gray evidently was in a minority and had to
subscribe to the majority report. His methods did not find
favour with the majority of the Council. He complained,
in another letter (31 Oct.) to Cromwell, that he could not
effectually serve the King without greater confidence being
placed in him, and mentioned the interference of Brabazon,
Agard, Pole, Cusake, and Walter Cowley. The two men that
he trusted were Chief Justice Aylmer and John Alen, Master
of the Rolls. They had previously pressed for his appointment as Lord-Deputy. Gray says that they seem honest
men, but Brabazon tried to make trouble between him and
them. These men had evidently been reported to Cromwell
as favouring Gray rather than Brabazon, and they sent a
letter [2] to the Lord Privy Seal to show that they were not
opposers of Brabazon : " According to your command to
us and Master Treasurer of the Wars, since the coming of the
army into Ireland we have always kept company together
from place to place. Irishmen were never in such fear as
now.

[1] *Cal. S.P.I.*, p. 20.   [2] *Carew Cal.*, p. 80.

" I, Aylmer, have received by the Master of the Rolls your letter, willing the Master of the Rolls and me ' to persevere in our old amity with Master Treasurer, and to join in one conformity ' to serve the King."

Agard, Cromwell's servant, was in touch with both parties, hearing their complaints against one another and reporting them to Cromwell. Aylmer and Alen complain of this in a letter [1] to Agard (28 Dec., 1535), in which they say : " You must be aware that hitherto we and Mr. Treasurer [Brabazon] have joined in one conformity to serve the King according to Mr. Secretary's pleasure. Both you and Mr. Treasurer have had our good hearts for Mr. Secretary's [Cromwell] sake, nor did we breathe a word of displeasure towards Mr. Treasurer but for your cause and by your conveyance ; for we knew nothing of your secret working toward both parties till we left Dublin ; whereat we can but marvel as we were always glad to report your will to Mr. Secretary. And if in discharge of our consciences to the King we had said anything to Mr. Secretary, you had no right to make yourself privy thereto. ' Remember what ye said to my lord Leonard in the garden at St. Sepulchre's.' As to your statement that either of us would have put Mr. Treasurer from his office, and advised you to labour for it, even if it were true it was not half honest in you to disclose it, but we will prove it false, and come to Mr. Secretary for the declaration of our honesty."

It is interesting to read what Martin Pelles has to say of these men and of the condition of the country. In a letter [2] to Cromwell (4 Dec., 1536), he says : " The saying of all the country is, that the changing of so many deputies has been the chief hurt of this land. It is a year or two before a new deputy becomes acquainted with the condition of the Pale and of the Irishry. . . .

" Mr. Treasurer is very well beloved, is a good justiciary, favourable to the common weal, and very hardy in the field. . . .

" The Master of the Rolls [Alen] is a man of great capacity and good wit in compassing any of the King's causes, and favours the poor people. . . .

[1] *L. and P. Hen. VIII*, vol. viii., no. 1027.   [2] *Carew Cal.*, p. 110.

" My Lord-Deputy has more discretion than he had when he came last out of England. He is also pityful to the poor people, and executes justice with charity, and without corruption, and is very ' painful, forward and hardy in the field.' "

In another letter [1] (6 Feb., 1537), he says : " If your Lordship do give command to the Deputy, the Treasurer, the Prior of Cellmaynam [Kilmainham] and the Master of the Rolls ' to avoid covetousness,' then the King and you will hear of such things done as will please you, which cannot be done so long as the Irishmen know as much of the King's counsel as the Englishmen who are the King's Council." In a further letter [2] (4 Dec., 1536), he says that the principal rulers should be native Englishmen ; for otherwise, if any of the lords of the Irishry came and rob within the English Pale, they will probably have friends among the rulers, and be able to make peace on returning a portion only of the spoil. Your Lordship should cause the Lord-Deputy, the Treasurer, and the Master of the Rolls " to be all three in one assent, above all other."

We cannot omit a reference to Walter Cowley's part in reporting the doings of the members of the Council. He was an underling of the Earl of Ossory, and was seeking his fortune by his adherence to the " reform." In a letter to Cromwell (10 June, 1536), he states that he " has forborne to write to Cromwell, knowing that other persons did ; that he is roughly handled for his truth, and untruly reported of in consequence of his refusal to bear tales against Mr. Agard. He trusts in Cromwell's judgment. He excuses Agard for not having written to Mr. Pole, and ' touched ' Alen and Aylmer. He was inflamed with excess of gladness at being restored to Cromwell's favour. The strife between them is beginning to rise again. Agard is known to be diligent, so that ' great mish should be of him.' He meddles not with Mr. Treasurer's praise ; but no one could soon stint in declaring his service, and he flees occasion of strife.

" Lately Ossory, the Lord Treasurer, the bishop of Meath, the lord of Kilmainham, and others, sent letters to Cromwell by Robt. Case, and they were opened by the Deputy and

---

[1] *Carew Cal.*, p. 115.　　　　[2] *Ib.*, p. 110.

others without Master Treasurer's knowledge.   Case is now in England, and can be examined.   He asks Cromwell to exhort the Deputy to leave such conduct.

"Nothing can be done until the army is out of debt, and no great power can continue unless the revenues are sufficient to pay for it.   The profits acquired by this Parliament will draw to a good sum.   A general reformation must consist principally in inhabiting, and in building and repairing defences.   Meanwhile the Deputy, with Ossory, Butler, and the English Pale, should endeavour to enfeeble the Irishry.

"He disapproves of the King's granting away the lands now had by this Parliament.   Those who make suit can be preferred to farms or other kinds that do not diminish the King's inheritance.

"Manors and castles in the Marches might well be given to hardy gentlemen in fee-farm.   Ossory and his son deserve as a reward the restoration of their old honor and inheritance which exceeds not £100 a year.

"He hears that his father [Robert] is like to have further preferment.   He must be exempted from any particular devises, and as having his only preferment by the King, to dwell among the Council here in Dublin, devising only the advancement of the King's affairs and profit." [1]

It is scarcely necessary to draw attention to the pleading for favour for his patrons the Butlers of Ossory and to that for his own father who was to be a kind of free-lance to report on every member of the Council " for the advancement of the King's affairs."

Gray had many enemies, for he was not conciliatory, and his relationship to the Geraldines laid him open to the suspicions of all who had risen on the ruins of the House of Kildare. With Brabazon, the ablest man about him, he had long been on cold terms, and many supposed that the Vice-Treasurer thought he himself ought to have been Deputy.   Thomas Agard, Vice-Treasurer of the Mint, a sour but apparently honest Puritan, hated Gray for his attachment to the old religious forms, and Browne lost no opportunity of attacking him on the same grounds.   Alen, Master of the Rolls, a useful public servant, but with an inborn love of intrigue, gave trouble

---

[1] *L. and P. Hen. VIII*, vol. x. *ad an.*

to every successive chief governor. Robert Cowley and his
son Walter were devoted agents of the House of Ormond
(Butlers), which Gray thought too powerful. The deputy did not
favour the innovations in religion, and took no pains to hide
his dislike of Browne and Agard ; but with the rest he was
always ready to co-operate.[1] Such was the Council that were
entrusted with " reform " in Ireland, men jealous and dis-
trustful of one another, seeking for promotion by fair and
foul means, and looking with avaricious eyes on the monastic
possessions, many of which they already held by lease from
the abbots and priors.

GRAY SECURES TREATIES WITH IRISH CHIEFS.

During the interval between the adjournment of Parliament (31 May) and its reopening at Dublin (15 Sept.) in
1536, Gray traversed the provinces and obliged the Irish
chieftains to subscribe to indentures of peace and submission
to the English Government. " In these indentures we find,
among the royal titles, that of the Supreme Head of the Church
of Ireland, but as yet no more explicit acknowledgment of
his supremacy. Nor are the stipulations on the part of
the Irish lords uniformly the same in all." [2] They simply

[1] See Bagwell, *Ireland under the Tudors*, i. 207-8.

[2] Leland, *Ireland*, ii. 168. *Rot. Can. Hib.*, 28 and 29 *Hen. VIII.* Cox
holds differently. He says : " It seems that the Lord-Deputy had new instructions to oblige all the Irish by indenture to own the King's supremacy, and to
renounce the Pope's usurpations, and to contribute something towards the
support of the Government, and to find a quota of men to every hosting." He
continues : " And so, on the 28 [June, 1537], he [Gray] came to Limerick,
where the Mayor and Aldermen took the oath of Supremacy, and swore to
renounce the Bishop of Rome's usurped authority : and the Bishop of Limerick
did the like, without scruple or hesitation : and order was left for the clergy and
commonalty of that city to follow that example, and that certificates of their
performance be returned into Chancery." He adds : " And on the 11th [July]
he came to Galway . . . and the Mayor and aldermen followed the example of
Limerick, and took the oath of the King's supremacy, and renounced the Pope's
usurped authority. . . . And it is to be noted, that all those that submitted
were bound by indenture, as well as oath, to own the King's supremacy and to
renounce the Pope's usurpations ; but when the King had an account of what
was done, he answered by his letter to the Lord-Deputy, that their oaths, submissions, and indentures were not worth a farthing, since they did not give
hostages, and so it afterward proved " (*Hib. Angl.*, i. 252-3). All this is true
of the indentures made on later occasions, but on this occasion there is nothing
to show that the Irish chiefs were asked to renounce " the Pope's usurped
authority."

stipulated as to keeping the peace, or not harbouring rebels, or attending general hostings, or remaining true and faithful subjects of the King, or contributing to the support of its Government. Amongst the submissions received was that of Thady O'Byrne, "chief captain of his nation," which says nothing about renouncing the " Pope's usurped authority." It relates : " According to the award of the Earl of Ossory, and others indifferently chosen, it is agreed that O'Byrne, and all under his rule and power, shall be loyal and obedient to the King, his heirs and assigns ; he shall not adhere to the Irishry nor harbour any messenger or rebel of the King, and particularly of the ' O'Tooly's,' nor succour any of them flying to him for protection ; and at hostings, out of Leinster, send a banner with 20 horsemen and a proportionate number of footmen, according to the usage of his country, at his own charges, to proceed with the Justice or Deputy ; and in Leinster, shall attend at such times with the whole ' posse ' of his country ; also, in case of necessity, shall find and support 120 armed Irish footmen, called galloglaghes, for 4, 6, or 8 weeks, or 3 months and that all those conditions shall be inviolably observed, the castle of Symondswood is to be delivered into the hands of the Lord-Deputy." [1]

Lands on the marches of the Pale were to be let upon condition that the tenants should use the English tongue, English habit, and forbear from alliance or familiarity with the Irish (31 July, 1537).[2] It was proposed to Cromwell that five or six thousand persons, part soldiers and part husbandmen should be planted between Dublin and Wexford.[3]

Though the four commissioners who came over, namely, Sir Anthony Sentleger, Sir George Pawlet, Sir Thomas Moyle, and Sir Wm. Barnes, had been appointed by the King to inquire chiefly into the abettors of the late rebellion and to give a general pardon, yet they received a new order to let the march lands for a period of twenty-one years.[4] Aylmer

[1] Cal. Pat. and Cl. Rolls, Hen. VIII, etc., p. 46.

[2] In an abstract of the disorders and evil rule within the land of Ireland it is stated that all the English March borderers use Irish apparel and the Irish tongue, as well in peace as in war, and for the most part use the same in the English Pale, unless they come to Parliament or Council (Cal. S.P.I., 1509-1573 [Sept., 1537], p 32).

[3] Ib., p 27.	[4] Cal. Pat. and Cl. Rolls, Hen. VIII, p. 35.

and Alen were appointed to join them, and Gray and Brabazon to assist them.[1]

Robert Cowley, writing to Cromwell in 1537, says: " Balymore and Tallagh 'longing to the Archbishop of Dublin, standeth most for the defence of the counties of Dublin and Kildare, against the O'Tooles and the O'Byrnes, be it therefore ordered that the commissioners shall see such farmers or tenants there as shall be hardy marchers, able to defend that marches." We shall soon see what success the commissioners achieved in defending or letting the archiepiscopal and other lands between Ballymore and Tallaght. Browne wished to have nothing to do with these lands as he found them too troublesome. They had, as we have seen, been cut off from the Pale. Even the manor lands in peaceful north Co. Dublin seem to have been a burden to the Archbishop.[2]

SUBJECTION OF IRELAND.

As a military exploit Gray's journey through the provinces, attacking and forcing to peace the Irish chiefs, was by no means contemptible, but his critics at the time seem to have been right in thinking it useless. The settled policy had long been to reduce the tribes bordering on the Pale, and not to overrun districts which there was no hope of reducing and holding. Browne was one of the Council who signed a letter (10 Feb., 1537) sent to the King which set forth the plan for the reduction of Leinster.[3] The signatories recommended that the towns of Wicklow and Arklow, which already had good castles, be walled, and certain companies of soldiers be appointed to inhabit and colonise them. Castledermot,

---

[1] *Cal. S.P.I.*, 1509-1573, p. 28.

[2] *Cal. Pat. and Cl. Rolls, Hen. VIII, circa* 1538. He was granted " licence with the consent of the chapters of the Cathedrals of Holy Trinity and St. Patrick, to alienate to Patrick Barnewell, of Feldaston, Solicitor-General, all messuages, burgages, lands, and tenements in Balgeith, in the parish of Swords, 3 a. of meadow in ' le Brode Mede ' [Broadmeadow] in same parish, 50 a. of land near Wourganeston in Clonmethan parish, commonly called ' lez fyftie acres,' 1 burgage or tenement in Swerdes, lying between the holding of Patrick Uryell, on the north, and the street of Swerdes, on the east, a park in the occupation of Ellen Hancoke, on the west, and a tenement of the said Archbishop, wherein Maurice Serjaunt dwells, on the south, and 13 a. in the west part of the Castell-felde in Swerdes. Rent for the premises in Balgeith and Wourganeston, £3 12s. 8d. Ir., and for the premises in Swerdes, 9s. Ir."

[3] *S.P. Hen. VIII, Ir.*, p. 414, *an.* 1537.

already a walled town, was to have another company. Certain gentlemen of England, " of good discretion," who had little or nothing to live on, should be selected so that they might give their whole attention to the lands granted them by the King in those Irish parts, and bring with them men who would settle down in the country. The colonisation of those districts would keep the Irish in check.

One of those impecunious gentlemen of England was to have Powerscourt, Fasagh Roe, Rathdown, and all Fercullen [1] for himself and his heirs. Another was to receive Castel-kevin and the Ferture [2] with money to rebuild the castle, unless the Archbishop of Dublin, to whom the castle belonged, should rebuild it and occupy it. Another was to be made Lord of Wicklow with a barony, and to have the district between Wicklow and Arklow, namely, the O'Byrne country, reserving to the King the ownership of the castle, the appoint-ment of the constable, the customs of the harbours, and the fee farm of the town. Another was to be made Lord of Arklow, with Inis-Kynshelan and other adjoining lands, comprising two baronies, reserving to the King the same rights as in the case of Wicklow.

All this looked very plausible, but to make it a reality required more than pen and paper. As usual the indefatigable Robert Cowley had plans of his own similar to those. The district from the Dodder to Bray was the debatable ground, favourably situated for the Irish attacks from the mountains above Glencree. It was thus desirable to have tried and true men to occupy the plains, especially about Shankhill. Accordingly, he recommended certain gentlemen, like Peter Talbot and the Walshes of Carrickmines, to occupy the dis-trict and resist the O'Tooles. Talbot was appointed Captain and Governor of the Harrold's country, with its castles and forts, instead of John Harold. [3]

---

[1] Fercualann was the territory from the crest of the mountains above Rath-farnham to Windgates between Bray and Greystones.

[2] Castlekevin, between Roundwood and Glendaloch, near Annamoe, was one of the Archbishop's manors. Ferture or Vartry was the district watered by that river, namely, from Roundwood down to Newcastle and Wicklow town. This was part of the O'Toole country.

[3] *Cal. Pat. and Cl. Rolls, Hen. VIII*, p. 26, 20 April, 1537. The Harrold country was the slopes of the Dublin mountains from above Rathfarnham to Shankill.

Having recommended stout marchers to have the castles
and garrisons in the Marches, Cowley advised that, on the
arrival of the King's commissioners for the subjugation of the
country, the Lord-Deputy, the Earl of Ossory, with the help
of the Palesmen, should negotiate with the Irishry on the
borders of the Pale and secure treaties until some time in
the following year when the King could set about in earnest
to reduce the whole land to obedience.   He was of opinion
that, if his plan were carried out, the English Pale, instead
of being 20 miles in length would be 200.   He warned the King
that except for the Butlers (his own great lords) and a very
few others, all the rest, Irish and Anglo-Norman chiefs, were
murmuring among themselves that the King intended such
a reformation that he would take no account of loyal or dis-
loyal subjects but would put them all together into, what
we now call, the glue-pot, and which Cowley called the
" hodgpot." [1]

On the very day (31 July, 1537) that Cowley wrote this
letter, the King issued instructions [2] to his commissioners,
Anthony Sentleger of Ulcombe, George Poulet, Thomas
Moyle, and William Berners, to suppress the Geraldines and
reduce the country to good order.

An interesting piece of information is given [3] in reference
to the reception of the commissioners by the Council in Dublin :
" This year there came to Dublin 4 commissioners instructed
with extraordinary authority whose names hereafter followeth,
Sir Anthony S. Leger, George Pallet, Tho. Moyle, Wm.
Barnes | men of the country and of the city | and they had
a noble dinner given them in Walter Tirrels house in December,
there sate in the midst of the table the Lord Deputy, and on
his left hand Sir George Brown Archbp. of Dublin, Sir Anthony.
St. Leger, George Pallet, the Bp. of Meath, the Prior of Kilmainham called Rowson, there sate without the table before
the Lord Deputy the Lord Chancellor called Barnwell, Lord
of Trimletston, and upon his right hand sate Thomas Moyle,
Wm. Barnes, on the right of the Lord Deputy sate the Baron
of Delvin, Wm. Brabazon, Tres. and John Allen Master of
the Rolles, and the left side of the Lord Chancellour sate the

---

[1] *S.P. Hen. VIII, Ir.*, i. 445, 31 July, 1537.   Letter to Cromwell.
[2] *Ib.*, ii. 452.   [3] *Loftus MSS., ad an.* 1538.

Lord Cheife Justice of the Kings Bench and next him Thomas
Luttrell Chief Justice of the Common Place, and next to him
Rich. Delahide Chief Baron of the Exchequer."

BROWNE ACCUSES BRABAZON OF FRAUD.

The jealousies and enmities existing among the members
of the Council of Ireland now grew more bitter, and more
disastrous to the project they had in hand.   Browne, for one
reason or another, found fault with the actions of almost
all the members of the Council in turn.   Indeed, he manu-
factured grievances and accusations, out of a desire to find
greater favour with Cromwell and as a set off against his own
failure to secure general acceptance of the Supremacy even
among his own diocesans.   Though at first in agreement with
Brabazon, he now sent to Cromwell certain accusations
against him.   In reply to these charges of fraud and peculation
against the Treasurer of the King's wars, Gray and Council
wrote [1] to Cromwell (30 April, 1537) :—

> To the right honourable
> The Lord Crumwell
> Lord of the private seale.

[Endorsed]

> The Council of Ireland
> for the discharge of Brabazon
> ultimo Aprilis 1537.

May it please your good lordship to be advertised that whereas
the King's deputy did write unto you of late how I was advertised
by some of the Council that Mr. Brabazon thesaurer [treasurer] of
the King's wars should deceive the King in diverse sums of money,
which for my discharge I signified unto you (as by the same way
my letters appeareth).   But to the intent that your lordship might
know the playnes [plainness] hereof, I with others of the Council
whom I have made privy of the same whose names be here unto
subscribed, have thought good to open unto the occasions whereupon we send writing principally proceeded.   The truth is that
the Archbishop of Dublin showed unto me against him both the
same and other things together with that expressedly and precisely that he [Brabazon] had beguiled the King in the account of
the receipts of his lands of the bishoprick above an Cl [£100].

---

[1] S.P. Hen. VIII, vol. iv., no. 22, P.R.O., London.

Which things he showed me first betwixt him and me saying that except I would advertise the King thereof he would accuse me to the King of the same. And after he declared the same matters to me the said deputy in the presence of part of us. Whereof both I advertised the same Mr. Brabazon, and, after having opportunity, others of the Council (whose names been subscribed). And we together remembering that the said Mr. Brabazon was one of the Council and put in high trust, and again considering that the other was an Archbishop and of the Council likewise : thought we could no less do than write with the same Archbishop therein. Whereupon in a secret faction [session] we called him to us for the same purpose. And to be plain to your lordship he cannot justify before us his saying against the said Mr. Brabazon, but in manner deemeth that even he spoke the same things. Which nevertheless undoubtedly he did divers times precisely affirm and say. And when we had heard this denial of him, and much marvelling thereof ; yet upon such privy knowledge as we had we objected unto him that we marvelled that he could deem that thing which (as we were informed he had written to the King or your good Lordship or to both). Whereupon he confessed that he had advertised your good lordship thereof. And therefore my lord we shall beseech you, that you suspend your credit both herein and all other such reports until the truth appear otherwise. For we perceive that by these particular writings and untrue reports, your lordship is not only oft disquieted, but also we hindered and blamed causeless. Wherefore, my good lord setting forth things apart, we beseech you eftesones for the love of God to have respect to our good wills and proceedings, and according thereunto to judge us. Repelling these seditious depravers of men's good doing ; whereby your lordship shall be greatly quieted ; and we highly comforted in our service, so knoweth God whom we heartily beseech to preserve your right honourable lordship in long and prosperous life. From Dublin the last of April.

Your Lordship's most assured,

> Leonard Gray.
> J. Barnewall, Lord Chancellor.
> J. Rawson, prior of Kyllmaynan.
> Gerald Aylmer, Justice.
> Patricke Fynglas, Baron.
> Thomas Lutrell, Justice.
> John Alen, Master of the Rolls.
> Thomas Houth, Justice.

Browne's underhand method of dealing with State affairs did not find favour with the Council. Whether he was right or wrong in his accusation, it was not a personal matter. It was the business of the Council to see to it. The accusation evidently turned on the profits of the temporalities of the See,[1] during vacancy, which were in the King's hands, and to which Browne had nothing to say as these were matters gone into before he came to Dublin. Browne's craftiness did not enhance his reputation, and the Council told him so very plainly. It is another example of the system of espionage deliberately fostered by Cromwell. It must, however, be remarked that Brabazon was not above suspicion. His accounts in connection with the suppression of religious houses later show him to have been lacking in honesty.

ACTS STILL UNPASSED. THE KING'S REBUKE.

Though many Acts had been passed in Parliament, others that were for the " King's advantage," namely, which would fill his coffers, were held up by the spiritual lords and their proctors in the Higher House and by other leaders in the Common House. These were the King's customs, the suppression of religious houses, the twentieths of all revenues, and probably the First Fruits. Robert Cowley, always on the alert to find favour with Cromwell, tells the whole story in a letter [2] to his patron (4 Oct., 1536) :—

My duty premised to your honourable lordship, as your most bounden orator. It might please the same to be advertised, that where certain acts were moved to have passed in the Common House here, one for a resumption of the King's customs,[3] cockets,

---

[1] Brabazon had entered the temporalities of the See from July, 1534, to Sept., 1535, as £623. Browne said they should have been about £723 (about £10,845, *1914 value*). In the thirteenth and fourteenth centuries they varied between £15,000 and £20,000 a year (*1914 value*), but in those days revenue was derived also from Ballymore, Castlekevin, and Shankhill manors.

[2] *S.P. Hen. VIII, Ir.*, i. 370.

[3] *Customs.*—In the time of Henry VII complaints were raised by alien merchants against navigation acts and customs duties. Besides export and import duties there were some twenty-four petty exactions by the officers of the King and of the municipalities. This King's policy was one of lavish encouragement to foreigners, dispensing them from the restrictive statutes. When Henry VIII came to the throne petitions were made by the English trading companies and gilds against alien trading. But the King and Wolsey held against them. According to Cowley's letter above it would appear that the

and poundage, into the King's hands ; the second, for the suppressing of certain religious houses, comprised in the King's commission sent hither for the executing thereof ; and the third, that
the King should have the twenty part of all the rents and revenues
of every man's lands during ten years ; which acts be yet rejected
in the Common House by the seduction of certain ring leaders
or belwedders, applying more to their own sensualities, singular
profits, and affections, than to any good reason or towardness to
prefer the King's advantage or commodity ; and have determined now to send into England two of the said house, such as
they think will hold fast, and stiffly argue to maintain their forward opinions, to vanquish the reasons of such, as would speak
in the King's causes ; to persuade, and if they could, inveigle the
King's council to defeat and reject the King's advantage and
profit by feigned suggestions. Of which two, Patrick Barnewall,
the King's Serjeant, is one principal champion ; who, and in effect
all his lineage of the Barnewalls, have been great doers and adher-
ents, privy councillors to the late Earl of Kildare.

We have already said that no minute has been found in
the State Papers which gives the particulars of the commission issued to Aylmer and Alen for the Parliament of
1536.   But Cowley is quite definite in stating that the
Suppression of Religious Houses was amongst the Acts to be
passed, and that it was thrown out in the Commons by the
influence of such laymen and lawyers, ringleaders, like Patrick
Barnewall. This champion and another were despatched by
their party to the King to show that, even though they had
admitted the King's supremacy, they did not grant that the
King had in law any right to suppress but only to reform
religious houses. They were also opposed to imposing any
taxation on the people in the way of extra customs duties,
the twentieths of revenues, and the First Fruits of ecclesiastical
offices. The country was sufficiently poverty-stricken as not
to be able to bear this undue taxation for the King's " advantage," namely, his wars and his pleasures. Cowley was

Dublin community were also in favour of reviving the duties against alien
trading.
     Cocket, or *coket*, was a document drawn up by the customer from the declara-
tions of merchants exporting goods.   It was the duty of the searcher in the port
of export to search the goods when on shipboard, and verify by aid of *cocket*
the consignor's declarations. *Cocket-money* was the fee for the customer's certificate of payment of export duties.

intent on the King's " advantage " with a view to his own advantage.

These Acts remained in abeyance during the winter, and the King's decision was evidently waited for.   Early in the year 1537, a report was spread that Lord Thomas Fitzgerald and his five uncles had been liberated and were returning to Dublin.   Lord Gray, in a letter [1] to Cromwell (4 Feb.), says that the Commons in the Parliament of Ireland were astonished at the report, and " the spirituality hath taken such an audacity, as it should seem, of the ruffle which hath been there, as they little regard to pass any thing."

The clergy evidently had begun to believe that with the return of the Fitzgeralds the question of the King as Head of the Church would sink into insignificance, as the cause of the Pope was identified with the success of the Fitzgeralds. Soon, however, this vain hope was to be shattered.[2]   A few weeks afterwards Henry wrote to the Council in Ireland (25 Feb.) telling them very plainly what his wishes were.

Amongst many important matters referred to in the letter, the King mentions :—

Seventh, you shall understand that it is much to our marvel, that you have not yet proceeded to the suppression of the monas- teries, and that you have had no more regard to our sundry letters written unto you for the alleviating of our charges there.   If you, that should be the advancers of our things there, will either in open Parliament hinder them, or be so remiss in the execution of them, when we be once entitled, that all men may see you proceed but for a form, against your minds, you do your parts but evil towards Us ; and we would you should all think that we have such a zeal to the advancement of the good of that country, that like as we

---

[1] *S.P. Hen. VIII, Ir.*, i. 407.

[2] As a matter of fact the day before (3 Feb.) Gray wrote his letter to Crom- well, Lord Thomas Fitzgerald and his five uncles were executed at Tyburn. Chapuys, in one of his letters to the Emperor, says that Henry would readily have sent Thomas back to Ireland in the hope that a rebellion might be started so that he could annihilate the whole Fitzgerald tribe.

The preservation of the House of Kildare is in a great measure due to Thomas Leverous, who was tutor to Gerald, brother of Thomas.   Gerald was, by the aid of Leverous, sent abroad until Edward VI (1552) restored to him the greater part of his estates, and Mary (1554) restored him to his titles.   Leverous was appointed by Mary dean of the restored chapter of St. Patrick's, Dublin, and, shortly afterwards, Bishop of Kildare.   (See Harris, *Ware's Bishops*, 390.)